'This is a tale of compassion with legs... It will challenge you to live such a life and encourage you that the place of our weakness and utter dependence on God is the place where we see miracles.'
Rev Mike Pilavachi, Senior Pastor at Soul Survivor, Watford

'The story continues to amaze me. It also encourages me to think of what God can do through anyone who believes they have heard God's call and is willing to respond in obedience to him.'
Bishop David Pytches, founder of New Wine

'As I read this book I couldn't help thinking of Charles Dickens's Scrooge, who declared, "I will live in the past, the present, and the future ... I will not shut out the lessons that they teach." Scrooge's life changes: instead of grasping, now he is giving. Instead of being bitter, now he is loving. Instead of being indifferent to the needs of others, now he is caring. His life is transformed, as ours should be, from humbug to hallelujah!'
Canon J. John, author and evangelist

'This is a book about Faith, Courage and Passion. It demonstrates how we can all touch the lives of others and the amazing impact we can all have when we see the potential in fellow human beings. This should be mandatory reading for those who work in the field of homelessness – it proves what can be done with so little.'
Nigel Parrington, Chief Executive, Salvation Army Housing Association

'Having seen at first hand the tremendous work of New Hope I am aware of just what a remarkable story it has been. This book chronicles that journey, and this latest edition reminds us it is a story which is still unfolding. I commend this inspirational book to you as a testimony to what can be achieved when we step out in faith to follow God's call to help those in need.'
Rev Tony Rindl, Rural Dean & Vicar of St Mary's Watford

'New Hope does what it says: it gives new hope to those in our town who are homeless and often without a purpose in their lives. It is a good thing that there is an organisation in our town that cares for our

D0231266

residents in need and where there is always somebody to talk to and somewhere to go.'
Dorothy Thornhill MBE, Elected Mayor of Watford

'Our support of New Hope over many years has been born out of their sheer commitment in supporting those whose life experience has resulted in them hitting rock bottom. The charity and its volunteers' commitment to these people is life changing for their service users and I therefore commend New Hope to anybody who is interested in seeing the lives of people who are vulnerable being transformed.'
Gary Grant, Managing Director, The Entertainer

'The work of New Hope has achieved huge practical benefits for some of the most vulnerable and troubled individuals in Hertfordshire. Many lives have been rebuilt and hope restored and I wish New Hope every success in its ongoing work, and hope it will continue to go from strength to strength.'
Louise Casey, Director General, Troubled Families

'A powerful and inspiring account of the birth and survival against all odds of a unique institution in our town (Watford), dedicated to giving hopeless cases new hopes and fresh starts. This book will touch the heart and soul of all those who share a common interest in valuing human dignity and giving a second chance to anyone unfortunate enough to end up homeless or destitute through circumstance rather than design.'
Councillor Rabi Martins, Watford Borough Council

'I always saw New Hope as a miracle – starting with such small beginnings in the tower of St Mary's Church, one night a week, and growing into what it is now – the main provider of services to the homeless in south-west Hertfordshire. Over the years it has touched so many lives, and met great human need; but it has been much more than that, because through the Trust the love of God has been shown and shared by those who have given so much to others. God was in this from the beginning; He has inspired and guided the work over the years; and He is glorified in all that has been achieved.'
Rev John Woodger, former vicar of St Mary's, Watford

Entertaining Angels

The Story of New Hope

Janet Hosier
and Liza Hoeksma

instant
apostle

Dedication

To all the angels who have passed our way –
many of whom are sadly no longer with us.

Do not neglect to show hospitality to strangers, for by doing that
some have entertained angels without knowing it.
Hebrews 13:2 (NRSVA)

First published in Great Britain by David C. Cook in 2007. This edition published by Instant Apostle, 2015.

Instant Apostle
The Barn
1 Watford House Lane
Watford
Herts
WD17 1BJ

British Library Cataloguing-in-Publication Data

A catalogue record for this book is available from the British Library

This book and all other Instant Apostle books are available from Instant Apostle:

Website: www.instantapostle.com

E-mail: info@instantapostle.com

ISBN 978-1-909728-26-4

Printed in Great Britain

Instant Apostle is a new way of getting ideas flowing, between followers of Jesus, and between those who would like to know more about His Kingdom.

It's not just about books and it's not about a one-way information flow. It's about building a community where ideas are exchanged. Ideas will be expressed at an appropriate length. Some will take the form of books. But in many cases ideas can be expressed more briefly than in a book. Short books, or pamphlets, will be an important part of what we provide. As with pamphlets of old, these are likely to be opinionated, and produced quickly so that the community can discuss them.

Well-known authors are welcome, but we also welcome new writers. We are looking for prophetic voices, authentic and original ideas, produced at any length; quick and relevant, insightful and opinionated. And as the name implies, these will be released very quickly, either as Kindle books or printed texts or both.

Join the community. Get reading, get writing and get discussing!

Contents

Introduction

I only have one memory of my mum in a wheelchair. It was in the last week of her life, a year after the first edition of this book first came out. Though her body was wasted by the combination of cancer, chemo and radiotherapy, she was adamant that she wanted to get out of the hospice, if only for an hour. I watched while nurses loaded her into the chair, carefully padding out the acres of space between her bony limbs and the chair's metal frame. When it came time for me to push her, the chair was horribly light.

But that afternoon remains one of the best of the final memories I have of my mum, Janet Hosier. I zigzagged her down Watford high street, steering as she directed us towards old friends and acquaintances, wheeling from one conversation to the next. I'm sure she knew that this would be the last time she'd do such a thing, and she seemed to relish the opportunity to give out words of encouragement so freely. 'Keep on trusting God,' she'd say. 'He's not giving up on you, so don't give up on Him…' and 'Make sure you treasure your wife!' If it hadn't been for the fatigue, she could have stayed out there all afternoon.

This kind of confidence and love of people was typical of Mum, but it hadn't always been. There had been times in her life when she felt timid, times when her worries about what people might think caused her to retreat and hide. But that was a long time ago, and the Janet who struggled to make it as a single mother was different from the Janet who ended up writing this book. So different, in fact, that I'm convinced anyone who lost touch with her before she turned 40 would struggle to recognise the woman she became.

While some of us get ground down by disappointment or become cynical, cold or narrow-minded, Mum's experience of and appetite for life got better and better as the years ticked by. The wonderful truth is that she achieved in her life what so many marathon runners aim for when they race: it's called the negative split. It means running the first half slower than the second, giving yourself time to find a pace and then improve on it, leaving enough in the tank so that you can finish strong, knowing that you gave everything you had in those final miles.

That's what she did – the negative split. She faced plenty of trials in her life, like we all do, and as the years went by she became increasingly determined not to be defined or distracted by them. Instead, she aimed to finish strong, to get better and better at being the person she believed she was created to be. In a word, she became more and more free.

One outlet for all that freedom took the form of her work with two friends, Sheila and Tim, to establish what was then called Watford New Hope Trust. The three of them knew that they simply couldn't walk past the homeless men and women who sat outside the town centre church. Even though it seemed as though almost everybody else was happy to ignore the local homeless, Tim, Sheila and Mum couldn't pretend that these people didn't exist. They couldn't cross over to the other side of the road. They had to do something.

It's a strange kind of freedom that compels a forty-something housewife like Mum to want to help people who are homeless. For many of us, freedom at that stage of life would look entirely different: we'd take more holidays; we'd spend our money on the luxuries that we'd always wanted; we'd hold on a little tighter to the things that are precious to us.

What Mum did wasn't unique – there are plenty of other good men and women out there who have done more – but in her story we find a brilliant example of what true freedom looks like. It doesn't leave us with our fingers clenched tight around the things we fear that we might lose. True freedom opens our hands and leads us to be generous with what we have, not to try to hoard it.

Right now, in your own hands, you hold the story of what happened when Mum, Sheila and Tim decided to let go of things that many of us find hard to release: money, reputation, safety and social comfort. It's the story of how they, like so many people from local churches in anonymous villages, towns and cities all over the world, made a choice to put their faith into action and start making a practical, tangible difference to the lives of the very people that the Bible tells us to care for.

New Hope has grown to become one of the largest homelessness charities in the home counties. Its holistic approach has won it fans in high political office and local government alike. It has made it possible for volunteers to know that they are making a difference, and it has constantly evolved to meet the changing needs of those who lack a stable, secure home.

They say that a great story needs to be both uniquely personal and wholly universal, that it needs to be different enough to inspire us but not so out-of-this-world that we can't relate to it. Read the rest of these pages and I hope you'll agree that *Entertaining Angels* has a bit of both.

What this book, as well as the staff and volunteers and supporters of New Hope, has shown over the years is that there is freedom to be found in being consistently generous. When we move beyond putting our hands in our pockets only when we feel sufficiently guilty, we find that we were made for more than just 'doing our bit' or offering 'the least we could do'. We were created in the image of an overwhelmingly generous God; is it really so surprising that the truly generous people among us are usually also the happiest?

I hope that as you read this book you will do so with both eyes open – one enjoying the story of a woman who discovered that she had more stamina and influence than she ever imagined, and the other tracking the way that generosity really does lead to the best experience of life. Don't put Mum on a pedestal; instead, let her story be like one of those little gifts of encouragement that she so loved sharing on that day I wheeled her down the street. Wherever you are on your own journey, I pray you'll put this book down feeling encouraged and inspired to take the next step towards a better, bigger life.

Craig Borlase

1: Do you know where you are going?

Therefore, if anyone is in Christ, the new creation has come: the old has gone, the new is here!
2 Corinthians 5:17

It was a sunny July day in the long, hot summer of 1976 and I was sitting beside the swimming pool in one of my new friends' back gardens. The lawns around us were perfectly manicured, the water was shining invitingly and our kids toddled around happily with colourful drips from melted ice lollies sticking to their bare skin. The scene was idyllic, yet my heart was heavy and filled with sadness. I didn't fit in here; this wasn't my world. I came from a working-class family where for many years we shared one bedroom with just two beds – one for my mum and dad and one into which my brother, my sister and I all squeezed. Our weekly treat was a finger each of Kit Kat, eaten in bed on a Sunday morning. For most of my life I'd felt just a little bit different from other people, as though I was never quite good enough. Here I was now, a 33-year-old single mother, struggling with all kinds of insecurities and carrying all sorts of baggage from my messy past, and yet my new friends, with their lovely homes and stable family lives, invited me in as though I was one of them.

My friend Pauline turned to me. 'Are you a Christian, Janet?' I shook my head. 'Do you want to be?'

I had been sitting on the fence for a while, but at that moment I cried to God from my heart, 'I've made such a mess of my life, now I give it to You to do whatever You want with it.' To be honest, I had no idea whether God could really make anything of my life and even what that might look like if He did. All I knew was that I was desperate for something in my life to change.

14

My first brush with religion was when I was three years old and my sister and I were sent to a convent. My dad had pneumonia and my mum had just given birth to my brother (we had been ill and were sent away to convalesce). The nuns were kind to us; they gave us Ovaltine sweets, which were a wonderful treat in our eyes, and they told us about Jesus. I can't remember exactly what they said, but I know I misunderstood it, as for a long time I believed that Jesus lived in the huge glass baubles that hung from the ceiling!

My family said grace before every meal, but it was part of the routine and, although my dad bought picture Bibles for my sister and me when we were young, we never talked about God. While we always felt loved and there were some very happy times, life was quite hard for our family. Our financial worries took a toll on my mum, she had a crippling fear of death, and the two things combined to drive her into a deep depression. I'd rush home from school at the end of the day and find that she was still in her dressing gown, huddled in a chair. The council house in which we lived was always a mess – Mum never had the energy to tidy or clean up and we were too young to do much about it. I hated it, though. I was never allowed to invite friends home and would never have wanted them to see where I lived. I was embarrassed about all the dirt and junk that littered the floors. My greatest dream was to have a magic button I could press and suddenly all the mess would be gone and I could be proud of my house and let my friends come round like the other kids! I hated the rows, too, standing between Mum and Dad to try and stop them. The arguments would often end with Dad throwing his dinner on the floor and storming off to work.

In our teenage years, as finances got better, things improved. The house was tidied up and our friends were made welcome. My dad was a great host and loved a drink, but Mum often went upstairs to bed, unable to face the company. Her mum had died when she was very young and her dad had remarried. She'd had the classic 'wicked stepmother' who abused her and her sisters and brother emotionally and physically, once kicking Mum down the stairs. Mum lived for us children and was determined to give us all the love she never had, but she was facing a tough battle against the pain she had experienced. Depression is a hard thing for many adults to understand, let alone children. Now I can see why life was so hard for her, but at the time I resented that she wasn't like all the other mums.

It wasn't only family life that made me feel different from the others at school; I had big teeth which stuck out and earned me the nickname 'Rabbit'. It was never said with malice, just kids being kids, but it really hurt at the time. My best friend through most of my school years and after was Diane, and she was gorgeous. With her long, light-brown hair, perfect features and coquettish ways, all the boys instantly turned their heads when she went past and I didn't stand a chance. I couldn't take much consolation from my brains either. I didn't enjoy school very much and sobbed my heart out on my mum's lap as she consoled me when I failed my 11-plus exam. That sense of failure stuck with me and seemed to permeate many areas of my life in the years to come; I always felt I wasn't good enough. Much to my astonishment and my parents' delight, I was made head girl, but I still left school with only two GCSEs – in Religious Studies and Cookery.

When my sister got married and my brother and I were working, Mum no longer felt needed and she was eventually admitted to a mental hospital when her depression took a turn for the worse. Dad was working late shifts and it was down to me to make sure his dinner was waiting on the table when he came in at 10.30pm I was exhausted and frustrated; life felt so unsettled. Given the lack of stability at home and my dreadful insecurities, it was no surprise that when a good-looking guy started showing interest in me, I fell hook, line and sinker.

His name was Tom, and he had the dark, brooding features of Dirk Bogarde and a snazzy sense of style. I couldn't believe he had picked me! I was in love for the first time, but even then I was confused: did I love Tom, or was I in love with the idea that he had picked me? His family couldn't have been more different from mine – they owned their own house, which was always immaculate, they didn't want for money, and they took holidays together (something we were rarely able to do in my family). When Tom and I got engaged his family invited me to go with them to the Norfolk Broads. We had a great holiday, it was relaxed and fun, and I felt as if I fitted in. When reality struck and the holiday came to an end, I struggled to go back to my own family. I was becoming a snob. I was so desperate to fit in and to have the luxury and security that money offered at last. I wanted what Tom's family had and I started to turn my back on my own family, to the point where I wouldn't invite my mum to come and get my wedding dress with me. If the truth be told, I felt ashamed of her.

Our engagement lasted for four years and even right up to the day of the wedding we both had our doubts that we were doing the right thing. Tom was an only child, used to being pampered and adored by his mother. He found it incredibly hard to leave home and I automatically slipped into the role of his mother, nurturing him in his insecurities. Together we bought our first home, in Essex – a modest new town house with a garage, but it was my first taste of security. The excitement of owning our own home eclipsed even the excitement of being newlyweds. I couldn't believe we had such riches. Tom was a photographer working in London and I worked in a local bank. Although we were both 22 when we married and thought we were pretty grown up, we were very immature and our marriage was empty from the beginning. The trouble really hit when I realised that while I was desperate for a baby, all Tom was interested in was sports cars. He loved them with a passion, always wanting to drive something that would make people turn their heads as he went past, whether it be a little MGB, a Marcus or a TVR. The list was endless and his passion was all consuming.

Things got so bad between us that eventually I said I wanted to leave. 'What would the neighbours say?' he asked, shocked at the idea. To me, the neighbours talking was the least of all our worries. But he talked me round, and I stayed. He even started to talk about having the baby I longed for, but we never did.

At around this time I took up driving lessons and my instructor, Michael, was everything Tom was not. He was good fun, a great communicator, educated and had a passion for reading. I felt so happy around him and really looked forward to seeing his white Ford Fiesta pulling up, signalling the start of my lesson and our hour together. As we got closer I realised this was more serious than just enjoying his company: he made me feel fulfilled in a way that Tom never had. We had fun and chatted as if there was no tomorrow. Suddenly I felt truly alive for the first time in my life, and so I left my husband after five years of marriage to be with Michael.

At first things were great. He was fun and gregarious, he shared his love of literature with me and spent hours reading me poetry. We started off living with his mum and then, when Tom and I sold our house, we moved out and rented a place of our own. With the extra cash from the sale, Michael took some time off work and soon our debts began to mount up. He became increasingly unhappy and restless, wanting to go to America to find some long-lost relations. I thought that would help release some of his frustration and hoped that when he returned he would have more energy to invest in our relationship. It didn't work. We carried on living far beyond our means. We moved from the farmhouse into a very smart – and therefore far too expensive – cottage. We bought a Rover and entertained extravagantly, and the money from the house was slowly disappearing.

Despite the state of our relationship and the financial worries, I was completely overjoyed when I found out I was expecting a baby. I had longed for a child for so long and my dream was coming true. Michael seemed happy too, but the responsibility was more than he could cope with. We talked about names: I liked Barnaby; he liked Craig. I gave in, eager to please as usual, only to find out much later that it was the name of his ex-girlfriend's son.

Craig was born on the 16th December 1972, and it was the happiest day of my life. Michael adored him; he was so proud of his son. He had been due on Christmas Day but I had hoped he would arrive early, as Christmas babies were big news in the local paper and I didn't want all that attention. Michael and I were not married but were known as Mr and Mrs Borlase as we did not want people to know we were having a child out of wedlock. We worried that if the truth came out we would be asked to leave by our landlady and would be too ashamed to face everyone.

We were in dire straits. Often Michael would not turn up for his driving lesson and I would receive a phone call from an irate pupil. He always had an excuse – the car had broken down, or he had run out of petrol. It looked as if we would not be able to pay our rent for very much longer. The idea of having our home taken away was devastating, particularly having a small baby. I did all I could. I spent hours breaking my back to deliver free papers for a few pounds a week and going from house to house to sell encyclopaedias. All to no avail. We could not pretend any more. All our debt caught up with us and we had to humble ourselves and ask my mum if we could live with her. The daughter who had left so proudly to get married and live a better life was now arriving back at the age of 31 as she had no money to pay her rent.

I spent my days working as an administrator and general dogsbody at a printing company and worked nights as an auxiliary nurse at Mount Vernon Hospital, to try and pay off some of our debts. I barely saw Michael and missed Craig desperately. I was exhausted from working so many hours, and yet the wages seemed to be gone before they made even a tiny dent in our mountain of debt.

One night I was clearing out Michael's suit pockets and found a note: he was having an affair with a woman at work. The shreds of my already tattered world came crumbling down. When I confronted him, he showed no remorse and he left shortly afterwards to be with her and her two children. I was devastated, and in my grief and anger vowed never to allow anyone to hurt me like that again.

Despite the pain, I could not regret having met Michael, as our relationship gave me my wonderful son who was the one good thing in my life. My mum and dad were good to me, but I was extremely conscious of not being a burden to them. I knew I needed to take drastic action if I was ever going to pay off my debts and get my life back together.

For some unknown reason I bought a copy of *The Times* (the newspaper of choice in our household was usually *The Sun*!), and there I saw a small advert from someone wanting a nanny and housekeeper in Chorleywood – a pretty, sleepy village in Hertfordshire. The one thing I still owned was an old green Hillman estate, so I drove myself to the interview. As I pulled up in the driveway of the beautiful four-bedroomed house, my car coughed and spluttered and I feared they would not want someone like me working for them and embarrassing them in front of the neighbours.

But Frank, who had placed the advert, soon put me at ease. Although he worked at the House of Lords, he was very down to earth. He needed a nanny for his two children – four-year-old Susie and seven-year-old Kate – as their mother had recently passed away. The interview went well, Frank and I got on straightaway, and the children were lovely. I fell in love with the house too: in spite of the sad circumstances it felt like a happy and peaceful home. Just as I was about to leave, Frank asked me if I was a Christian. I found it an odd question, but told him truthfully that I was not, but I did believe in a force of good and a force of evil. This seemed to satisfy him and he offered me the job.

I worked hard to clear the debts Michael and I had accumulated and enjoyed living and working with Frank and the kids. Susie and Kate thought Craig was great – he was a toddling 15-month-old and they thought he was a real live doll for them to play with, so they all got along really well! But I was like a fish out of water, a working-class, struggling single mum, thrown into a middle-class lifestyle full of what I perceived as very 'together' people. I would get invited to dinner parties as Frank's guest and felt totally out of my depth. I was embarrassed every time I opened my mouth, as my Essex accent clearly marked me out from the other well-spoken guests. What could I talk to them about? I had nothing in common with anyone and I would rehearse what I would say before the dinner, only to be mute for the majority of the evening, just wishing it was time to go home!

Although I had a stable job and we were living in a lovely house, the pressure of bringing up Craig alone (his dad felt his responsibilities now lay with his girlfriend's children rather than with his own son) and the disappointments and pain from my past were weighing heavily on me. I had such an inferiority complex and excruciatingly low self-esteem that if someone I knew was walking down the road, I would keep my head down and cross to the other side to avoid having to talk to them.

On a routine appointment at the local dentist I saw a Christian leaflet in the waiting room which asked, 'Do you know where you are going?' The question began to haunt me. I had no idea. All I knew was that my life was a mess, and had it not been for my son I would have wanted to take my own life. For the first time I was forced to realise just how desperate I had become and I did not know which way to turn.

I went to my doctor and he prescribed me antidepressants. Thankfully he knew that I needed more than just medication, and he also put me in touch with a single parents' group. The women who ran it were so kind. I could not get over the fact that they were living in their lovely houses, with stable family lives, and yet they accepted me – a screwed-up, neurotic, don't-know-how-I've-made-such-a-mess-of-my-life single parent – without question. They invited me into their homes and into their lives. Their warmth and kindness made a huge impact on me at a time when I was struggling. They loved me without question when I could not even love myself.

I was overwhelmed by their kindness, but when one of the women, Janet, started talking about Jesus, I was not ready to hear it. 'I love spending time with you, but please don't talk about all that religion stuff,' I said, but she did not let up easily. She told me how much God loved me and that He could make a difference and give me a fresh start.

I was also gradually making other friends in the community, mainly through Frank. Through his job he mixed with lots of cultured people and I just felt like Eliza Dolittle in comparison. Still crippled by my Essex girl accent, I eventually saved up my precious wages and paid for elocution lessons so that I would fit in better. It seemed costly to learn to say 'The cat sat on the mat', so I soon gave up, but the tutor did teach me to say 'anything' instead of 'anythink', which helped a bit when I was trying to impress! One night we even had a lord over to visit, and I spent the whole day beforehand in my room rehearsing things I could say to him that would make me sound intelligent. I was so terrified that I would say something stupid and show Frank up that I barely said a word and could not eat.

At around this time I met a lovely man from a neighbouring village and we became romantically involved. He was a great friend, a good man and a great role model for Craig. He introduced me to opera and wanted to share all the good things in life with me, rather than educate me like Michael had wanted to do. But there was an underlying sadness to our relationship: he was getting over a previous relationship and I was lonely and looking for some security. However, we enjoyed each other's company and, to anyone who saw us with Craig, we looked like an average family, even hiring cottages and spending our holidays together in Wales and Ireland.

I was still in touch with my parents, but only occasionally. One of the biggest regrets of my life is that I did not take Craig to see them more often. Being a grandmother myself now, I can understand the pure unadulterated joy you feel at seeing your children's children, and I wish I had realised at the time what it would have meant to them. One weekend, not long after we had moved to Chorleywood, I got a call to say that Mum had been taken ill and was in hospital. I decided to take Craig to go and visit her, and when they saw each other it was hard to tell whose smile was the biggest. Craig launched himself into my mother's arms and she squeezed him so tightly I thought she would never let go. We sat and chatted and she told me she was not afraid of dying now. She said to me, 'Don't regret anything,' and I cried as I told her how sorry I was for letting her down and not being the daughter I should have been. She looked at me with such love that I realised she did not feel as bad about me as I felt about myself. When I got the phone call the next day telling me she had died, I was devastated, but so grateful that we'd had that opportunity to talk, and that I had not left it too late to make my peace with her.

My friends from the single parents' group supported me greatly as I grieved, and they began to ask me to go to St Andrew's Church in Chorleywood. It surprised me to find that the church was full and buzzing with excitement. My heart thudded as I went through the door for the first time; I think I expected my life to be written across my face and that people would know I was not a believer and throw me out. I was relieved to find that I received nothing but warm smiles and a friendly welcome from everyone, including the vicar there, John Perry, who greeted me kindly as though I was already one of the family.

I carried on going to the church on Sunday evenings, as this was when I was off duty. I would sit at the back and observe. One week I sat next to an old gentleman with kind eyes who said to me, 'Are you a Christian?'

'I'm sitting on the fence,' I replied.

He nodded. 'It's the most uncomfortable place to be, isn't it?'

He was right. It was uncomfortable – but I felt comforted by his words, in a funny way. I left with that thought resounding through my head, wondering which way to jump. The same gentleman came to visit me the next day and offered me a book, *How to Give Way to Your Faith*. It described my struggle exactly – how to give way to believing that this good news was really for me, that Jesus had died for all the things I had done wrong. It was just a week later that I sat with my friend beside her swimming pool and offered all that I had to Jesus in the hope that he could turn my life around.

For a whole year I did not feel a thing – there was no emotion when it came to my feelings towards God. I went to church, I read the Bible and I prayed, but nothing seemed to go from my head down to my heart. It was as if there was a huge blockage, but I had no idea what to do about it.

Eventually I asked one of the ministers at St Andrew's. 'I'm trying so hard,' I said desperately, 'and nothing seems to make me closer to God.'

'Try relaxing,' came the wise advice. 'It sounds as if you've got spiritual indigestion!'

One of my biggest problems was forgiveness. I could not seem to get past all the things I had done in my life that had caused others pain. One week Barry Kissell (who was on the St Andrew's staff) spoke using the verse, 'As far as the east is from the west, so far has he removed our transgressions from us' (Psalm 103:12). At the end of each service they offered to pray and minister to anyone who was in need, and I knew that I needed to know the truth of those words deep in my heart. I went to the front and Barry came to pray for me. I could not grasp that these words could be meant for me; I had clung to my own sin for so long.

'Could God really forgive me?' I asked. 'For hurting my mum and dad and turning my back on them? For walking away from my marriage?'

'Yes,' Barry said firmly. 'As far as the east is from the west, that is how far He has removed your transgressions from you.'

As the tears flowed and I opened myself up to the love and grace of God, something dramatic changed inside me. For the first time I felt I could lift my head up high, I could look people in the eye and know that I was forgiven. If God did not judge me, then who else could? I no longer needed to live as though I was apologising to everyone. It felt as though I had been carrying a rucksack of bricks around with me and someone had finally taken it off.

I was beginning to realise that other things in my life needed to change. I was still seeing the same man and I grew restless in my spirit, wondering if I was supposed to end the relationship. We stopped things for a while and then just gradually drifted back to each other – there was a safety in the familiarity.

Friends advised me that it could not carry on – we had to break up or get married. I became unhappy, falling into the spiral of depression again, not knowing which way to turn. One cold November day, I felt it was all getting too much for me. I bundled myself up and took myself off to work in the garden, digging the hard earth ferociously to get out my frustration. With each movement I cried out to God, 'What should we do? Should we get married or not? Please speak to me, because I can't go on like this.'

That night he came round to see me and said he wanted to talk. He felt we had been drawn to one another largely due to our circumstances and should end our relationship. He was surprised at my reaction: I felt as if a huge weight had been lifted from my shoulders. It was as if I was being set free, and I knew God had guided us.

Although I knew it was the right thing, I still longed for someone with whom I could share my life – going to the theatre or to a concert, or just enjoying a meal together. I missed that kind of companionship.

My dad had remarried after my mum died and then tragically, only a year later, his new wife, Molly, died of a heart attack. Determined not to make the same mistakes as I had made with my mum, I devoted myself to looking after my grieving father. One Sunday, as I put a roast beef dinner on the table, the doorbell rang. It was Ron, Molly's son-in-law from a previous marriage, who had come to see how he was. I had to pick food quickly from each plate to gather enough for him to stay to lunch, but it was definitely worth it! A week later he took me to the theatre in Watford, and a few days after that we went for a walk in the local park. I did not want to start any kind of relationship by putting on a front and pretending to be something that I was not, so I laid it all out for Ron right there and then. As we walked, I told him everything from my past – all the mistakes, all the things I was ashamed off, everything.

To my amazement and delight, it did not put him off – in fact, he seemed even keener!

With this new relationship starting, I decided it was the right time to move out of Frank's house and rent a flat for Craig and me. It was very difficult to separate the children, who had grown to be like brother and sisters over the five years we were there.

A few months later, Ron came round with a beautiful single red rose and a note which asked me to marry him! I was over the moon, and on the 22nd December 1979 Ron and I married, less than a year after we had met. He was used to living on his own and was set in his ways, but we managed to make things work. At the time of writing, we have been married for 27 years and, like any marriage, it has not always been easy. In those early days we underestimated the impact of bringing two families together – Craig was now 7 and Ron had two sons from his previous marriage who were 10 and 14. We had not worked out a strategy for making this a smooth transition for everyone, but somehow we all muddled through.

In the following years, as life grew more stable, I carried on attending St Andrew's and God continued to heal me. I spent many hours weeping on the floor of the church over the pain of my past, allowing God into parts of my heart on which I had shut the door many years before, for fear of the overwhelming pain there. At last I was in what seemed to be a loving relationship and had a secure home, plus Craig was doing well at school and was finding a faith of his own.

When we moved to Watford in 1985, I started going to a church called St Mary's, so that I could be part of a local community of worshippers. It was here that I first got involved with a project to provide food for the local homeless people and met Sheila Meaning, who would be instrumental in setting up New Hope Trust with me. When my attention was drawn to the homeless guys who sat outside the church, I did not have a clue what would grow from the seeds God was planting in my heart. If he had given me an idea, I do not think I would have believed him. All I knew was that I was learning to listen for God's voice and to trust his direction – vital foundations for what lay ahead.

2: The Tower Club

For I was hungry and you gave me something to eat, I was thirsty and
you gave me something to drink, I was a stranger and you invited me
in ... whatever you did for one of the least of these brothers and sisters
of mine, you did for me.
Matthew 25:35, 40

There were a number of homeless guys who hung around
outside St Mary's, and I knew in my heart that if my faith
meant anything at all, then it had to mean something to them.
Although I have never lived on the streets, I have known the
loneliness of being on the outside many times, feeling as
though you are on the fringes and that you do not belong, so
my heart went out to them.

One guy in particular caught my eye. Every Sunday when I
went to church I saw him sitting on the small green outside,
building up a collection of empty cider bottles as he worked his
way through them. One day I knew that even though I felt a bit
nervous, I needed to go and say hello. His name was Pat,
known to his friends as Irish Pat, and he had bright, twinkling
blue eyes, a warm Irish accent and a polite and amusing
manner. As we chatted he told me he had been in prison, had
lost contact with his family and was now homeless, living in
the nearby car park with friends.

When we finished talking, he smiled, looked me in the eye
and said, 'Thanks.'

I felt embarrassed, conscious of all the help he needed and
what little I was able to offer him. 'For what?' I asked.

'Listening,' he replied. 'Most people don't want to know.' As
I walked away I was crying out in my heart to God for this man
who had found himself on the streets with no one to turn to.

Surely our faith had to have an impact on how we treated those outside the church, like Irish Pat and his friends.

'What else can we do?' became the prayer in my heart.

Little did I know that God was stirring other people as well. At around the same time as I was beginning to chat to the guys outside, Colin Bullimore, a member of St Mary's, went to Spring Harvest and was inspired by the work and teaching of Colin Urquhart, a vicar who had invited homeless guys to come and live alongside him. He read Colin's book to understand more and felt challenged to do something to help the guys he had seen outside the church. One morning he woke up and knew God was telling him to go to Tower Bridge, but he was not sure why. He called and explained to his boss at the Naval Headquarters in Northwood that he could not come in that day, and he and his slightly bemused wife Stella headed to London. As they walked over from the South Bank, unsure of why they were there and where to go next, they saw the London City Mission offices. They went in and spoke to the staff, who immediately sent them to their homeless centre in Covent Garden, which was run by an ex-homeless alcoholic and drug addict called Bush Hogg. Bush had come to know Jesus and set up the centre to help others in similar dire straits. As Colin spent time there, he understood what it took to set up a project to feed the homeless and grew in certainty that this was what God wanted him to do back in Watford.

Full of enthusiasm, Colin presented the idea to the congregation one Sunday, along with Noreen, another member of the church. Previously people had been reluctant to get involved with the local homeless people, but God had been changing many hearts and suddenly people were volunteering to help and offering money to get the initiative off the ground. As I listened, I grew more excited at the idea of having some practical way of helping these guys, and I offered my services straightaway.

In December 1987 the Tower Club was launched, taking its name from the area of the church dedicated to its use. The idea was to open our doors once a week to anyone who needed a meal and provide them with a hearty, nutritious dinner. There was a small team of volunteers who would cook, wash up, make cups of tea and sit and chat to the guys to make them feel welcome and get to know them. Noreen and Vera were our wonderful cooks, who would come up with feasts every Thursday night – sometimes meat, roast potatoes, lots of vegetables and a pudding. The menus were imaginative and appetising, paid for by donations from the church and sympathetic shopkeepers. Noreen worked at the local hospital and was used to the homeless turning up there, often the worse for wear, having got into a fight. She reminded me of an old-style matron, kind but firm, and the lads loved her. What a welcome change it was for the guys who came to sit down to a proper dinner. Many told us that for the rest of the week they suffered the humiliation of scavenging through bins to find a few scraps of food to sustain them.

I have to admit I was pretty naive when we began. On the first night, as I walked through the door, nervous about how the evening would go, the first thing I saw was a guy sniffing from a bag. 'What's he doing that for?' I asked a friend. Our first night, and I learned what glue-sniffing was – what a way to start! I began to wonder just what we had got ourselves into, but the evening went well and within weeks our 35 places at the table were filled. For some of the church volunteers it was a shock to come face to face with homeless people for the first time. Their dirty, unkempt appearances and loud manner could be alarming, but people usually found that as soon as they started chatting the guys were a friendly bunch, very appreciative of the church's efforts to help them.

As word got round, the numbers increased and we would end up eating in shifts. We always had enough food to go round, though, and when the meal we had cooked ran out there were sandwiches that our local Marks and Spencer and Boots had donated as they had reached their sell-by date. God always provided, whether it was through financial donations to buy food, or through goods given to us by local supermarkets. We even had a local business give us two 30-pound turkeys at Christmas – there was so much meat we did not know what to do with it all!

We had not been going long before I was presented with another first when one of the lads pushed a tiny stone into my hand while we were chatting outside the church.

'What's this?' I asked, looking at the small brown lump.

'A present,' replied Patrick.

I showed it to one of the other guys, Bob, in confusion, and he told me it was cannabis. I dropped it in shock and it rolled away, lost in the dark. It was one thing asking the guys to leave their bottles of alcohol on the doorstep before they came in, which they respectfully did, but quite another to have illegal drugs on the premises. I told Patrick we would report him to the police next time, as he was jeopardising the Tower Club for everyone else. He shuffled off shamefaced ... and never did it again.

I had never seen any illegal drugs before and I was shocked at my own naivety. I said to Bob, 'I really must go on a course to learn more.'

With a knowing smile, he said, 'Let's start now, Janet. What do you want to know?'

Bob was a long-term alcoholic and he told me how his father had raped him when he was just a small child and even invited his friends round to do the same to them. It was a betrayal of such a cruel and violent nature that Bob inevitably left home and found himself on the streets with only a bottle for comfort.

I later learned that the lad who had been sniffing glue that first night was called Gary. His parents had divorced and, while he had wanted to stay with his mum and be a part of her new family with his stepdad, she had wanted a fresh start – and that did not include Gary. That was one of the amazing, if heartbreaking, opportunities that the Tower Club presented – getting to know the guys and hearing the stories that had brought them to this place. There was no temptation to judge their situations or addictions when it became clear that they were not so different from us. Hearing story after story of painful and challenging circumstances, you could not help but think, 'If things had been different, I could have been sitting on the other side of the table; I could have been the one living on the streets.'

Billy Frost had one such story. He was a charming and gregarious Irishman who was always immaculately dressed, despite not having anywhere to stay. He had been married, owned a house and worked long hours building up a successful construction business, only to come home one day and find his wife in bed with a friend of his. Unable to cope with the pain, he drank away the money he had and ended up on the streets, addicted to alcohol. Many people think homeless people have chosen to be there or deserve it in some way, but the more we heard, the more we knew that was not true.

We learned a lot in those first few weeks and began to understand the code of ethics by which the guys lived. Some of them were brutal, with violent tempers. Although they did not drink on the premises, they often arrived in an alcohol-induced stupor, ready to blow at any point. One of the things that first struck me about Sheila, who was also volunteering at the Tower Club, was that even though she was not much over five foot and had just turned 50, she was not scared of breaking up a fight. If things kicked off, she would wade in. 'Come on, ducks,' she would say. 'There's no need for that in here.' And instantly the situation would be diffused. I admired that hugely, as I could not chastise anyone to save my life – the minute I tried, my heart would pound, my face would get taut and the words seemed to lose their impact.

Sheila and I began to work side by side and I got to know something of her past. She had grown up with an alcoholic mother and stepfather who fought violently. As the eldest of three sisters, she got used to being the one to try and calm things down and would get right in the middle as fights began. When I met her, Sheila was grieving the loss of her beloved husband Frank, to whom she had been married for 28 years. Frank had suffered a difficult childhood too: his mum used to lock him and his sisters in a room while she went out drinking. You would never have known it, though, to see how he was with their three kids. He was the most amazing father. He wanted to give Shirley, Alan and Perry everything he and Sheila had never had as children, and he worked hard to provide for them. He took them swimming all the time, taught them all himself, and they knew every corner of every park in London before they were ten years old.

When the kids grew up, things began to change. Frank did not feel needed any more and he took to drinking more and more and smoked heavily. He was never violent or aggressive; in fact, the main problem with him drinking so much was that he wanted to talk – all the time! He would get home from the pub and just want to chat away, while everyone else grew tired and wanted to go to bed. He said it was only social drinking, but having seen the effect of alcohol in her childhood home, Sheila was wary. Sheila had a real empathy with the guys who were homeless. She would see them on the streets and think, 'If I died, that would be my Frank huddling there in the shop doorway under that thin blanket.' Her children said she was being stupid to think that way. They said they loved him and would never let it happen, but she felt in her heart that it was true.

Frank needed something to kick him out of the rut into which he had got himself, and the only solution Sheila could think of was having a baby around again, as that always seemed to bring him to life. Not long after she had thought this, their 24-year-old daughter, who was unmarried and still living at home, told them she was pregnant. Some parents would have been horrified, as at that time having children outside marriage was not very common, but Sheila's first thought was an indication of her practical nature which was to serve us well in our work together: 'Where will we put the cot?'

Sure enough, having a new baby in the house slowed Frank's drinking. He loved to hold his grandson, Ben, and knew they would not let him if he had had a few. Wanting the baby to be baptised, they also started attending their local church, where Sheila was enveloped by the warmth and love she found there. As she heard more about what Jesus had done for her, she began to love, trust and follow Him.

Frank had been a fit, hard-working man who took pride in his job, and when one of his colleagues noticed that he was not functioning as well as he usually did, they were concerned. His boss sent him to the doctor and he was told to go straight to hospital. They kept him there for a week as they ran tests and Sheila visited him every day. Her strong husband was suddenly frightened, and he would rest his head on her shoulder and nestle in. 'It's my fault,' he would say. 'It's the smoking and drinking that's done it; it's my fault.' The truth was that it was asbestos dust from his job that had caused the cancer – the doctor said it had probably been growing for the last 25 years.

Sheila was working as the cook-in-charge at a local school at this time. One morning not long after she had been given the news of Frank's cancer, she was rolling out the pastry as normal when she heard a voice, although no one was with her. 'Frank's going to die, Sheila.'

She could not bear even the thought and cried, 'I don't want to hear it!' How could she believe that her Frank was going to die?

Again she took the practical solution and made an appointment to see the doctor. He confirmed their worst fears and said that Frank probably had two more years to live. Devastated at the idea of losing him, Sheila knew it was far worse to think of him slowly fading away before their eyes. The man who had always looked after his family could not bear to have them watch him die so dependent on them. Desperate, Sheila got down on her knees and prayed, 'God, would you take Frank? Don't leave him in all this pain with so much suffering to endure. Please take him peacefully.' God answered that prayer the very next day and took Frank in his sleep, leaving Sheila broken-hearted but assured of God's mercy and nearness.

Sheila and I both knew that the pain we had experienced in the past had given us a love for the guys at the Tower Club which was genuine. If we had looked on them as a project, they would have seen right through us and it would not have taken long for us to get jaded or for them to close off to insincere offers of friendship. Sheila also knew that the love and stability of family life had been what had saved Frank from becoming a homeless alcoholic after his traumatic childhood, and we wanted to offer what love and support we could to these guys who had been through so much and had no one to look out for them. We began to see there was also healing for us in that place of serving God. For Sheila, the guys were an extension of her family while she was grieving the loss of her husband, and I was about to go through some testing times with my health that made the work we were doing even more important to me.

The Tower Club had been going for a couple of years when I found what every woman fears: a lump in my breast. I was 45 at the time. The doctor did not seem to think there was anything to worry about, but sent me to a consultant to be sure. He too said he was 99 per cent sure that everything was fine – but I had a feeling it was not going to be as easy as that. Sure enough, when I came round from what was supposed to be a routine biopsy, they confirmed that it was cancer and told me that they had done a lumpectomy. The good news was that it had not spread too far, but it was enough for me to need six and a half weeks of radiotherapy. When they told me all this, I smiled and said, 'That's OK.' But hours later I broke down in my sister's arms, terrified of what the future would bring.

During my recovery I started to ask God what he wanted me to do. I could not carry on as I had before, involved in so many things going on at the church, as I did not have the time or the energy after my treatment. Apart from the prescribed drug causing a DVT (deep vein thrombosis, or blood clot), I was assured that the treatment had been successful. The following year, however, I started to have a pain in my ribs. It got so bad that I could not walk up the stairs. My greatest fear, of course, was that the cancer was back. Tests showed that it was not cancer, but a lung embolism. After the clot had been successfully dispersed, my doctor cheerfully told me that this condition had been potentially more life-threatening than the cancer!

The drugs they gave me forced me to spend even longer recuperating, which gave me more time to ask God what I should be focusing on. I felt him say quite strongly that the lads I had met through the Tower Club were to be my priority. Although more than aware of my shortcomings, I knew I could offer them friendship and love. It had meant so much to me that someone had loved me when I felt unlovable, seeing past the things that I felt made me an outsider and including me, and I was desperate to do the same for these guys. The lads were so pleased to see me and greeted me with reassuring

3: A home with heart

Is not this the kind of fasting I have chosen ...
to share your food with the hungry
and to provide the poor wanderer with shelter?
Isaiah 58:6–7

The guys lived for Thursday evenings. The Tower Club had been going well, and we had been able to serve a growing number of homeless men and women every week by moving from the Tower to the church centre. But some folk were growing increasingly unhappy. The church centre was also used for Scouts, Brownies and a nursery school, so after each Tower Club we would have to disinfect the whole area to make sure it was in a fit state for the next activity.

Sometimes the lads would come to church, but it was not always easy to integrate them into the congregation. With no fixed homes and no place to clean up, they often smelled quite bad, while some suffered from mental health problems or were drunk and would interrupt sermons and make inappropriate comments. Once a month the Tower Club coincided with the PCC meeting, and it always seemed to be that particular night when we would have trouble. Sometimes fights fuelled by alcohol and jealousy would break out, and for some reason they became more frequent when members of the committee were there to witness them. This was likely the catalyst to the PCC decision to close the Tower Club after the summer break in 1989.

Sheila and I were upset and angry. It was supposed to be the 'decade of evangelism' and this was the guys' only contact with church. We also knew that this was the only proper meal some of them were having and we could not bear the idea that they would not even get fed once a week. Recognising in each other the same conviction and determination, we went to the vicar, John Woodger, to see if he could keep it going. Despite our best protests, however, there was no going back. The church had been faithful for the past two years, but the decision had been made that it was time to pass the baton to someone else.

Sheila popped round one evening; we chatted and wondered what God's take was on all of this. We knew that God would be in control, no matter how things looked, and wondered how He would redeem the situation. We had no plan or strategy, no belief that we were up to the task, just a desire to continue helping the guys we had come to know. We knew the answer did not lie with us and as we started to pray, the words from Isaiah 58 leaped from the page:

> Is not this the kind of fasting I have chosen:
> to loose the chains of injustice
> and untie the cords of the yoke,
> to set the oppressed free
> and break every yoke?
> Is it not to share your food with the hungry
> and to provide the poor wanderer with shelter –
> when you see the naked, to clothe them,
> and not to turn away from your own flesh and blood?
> Then your light will break forth like the dawn,
> and your healing will quickly appear;
> then your righteousness will go before you,
> and the glory of the LORD will be your rear guard.
> (Isaiah 58:6–8)

'That's it,' we thought. The answer from God was that we were to invite the guys into our homes. Together we pondered the scripture, allowing it to sink into our hearts. Deep down we knew it was God. Even as we were asking Him, 'Is this really what you want us to do, Lord?' we were growing more convinced that God was calling us to be the answer to the problem.

Excitedly we went to see our vicar. We shared the scripture and he listened as we told him that we felt God was calling us to invite the homeless guys into our homes and feed them. His reply was wise and simple: 'If God has told you, you must do it. Just make sure you have a man around for safety.'

So we started planning evenings at my home. In our enthusiasm to keep things connected to the church, we asked the lads if they would like to learn more about God. We had decided to pick them up from the church, thinking that we could stay in control of when they came over if they did not know exactly where we lived. As I drove my little beige Panda up to the church car park, I looked around to see how many people had come, but there was no one there. I waited and waited and soon realised that no one was going to show. I went home despondent and talked to Ron about it. 'Why did you invite them to learn about God?' he asked. 'You wouldn't ask that of our friends. Why don't you just invite them for a meal and to watch a video?' He was so right. The next week we did just that, and this time we had enough guys show up at church to warrant two car trips!

I loved being able to open my home. It reminded me of all those times as a little girl when I had longed to be hospitable but was not allowed to invite friends in. Now we had a lovely house, right opposite an expansive park, and our own 300-foot garden, and we could welcome people who really needed a place to be. The house was a real gift from God. When Ron and I got married we were just able to buy a tumbledown house that needed lots of work. We did not mind, as it was our first home together, but after a few years we wanted to move nearer to our children's school. As this was in a nice part of Watford, we knew it would be out of our price range. Then I saw a house in the estate agent's window and it was at least £20,000 less than one would expect to pay for comparable houses. When I telephoned, however, it had gone. I let my disappointment out to God and felt him say, 'Just wait.'

A year went past and the same house came on the market again, just £10,000 dearer. I phoned the agents to ask what had happened. The agent explained that the owner had not been able to find the right house so had taken it off the market, but was now ready to sell again.

Excitement growing in me, I asked quickly, 'Can I see it?'

He laughed. 'There's not much point. I've had 23 people wanting to view it already!'

He kindly added me to the growing list, though, and I fell in love with it as soon as I walked through the door; it felt like home. It was so beautiful that all the viewings led to offers, some cash, others higher than the asking price, including one offer from a well-known Watford footballer! The owner, Mrs Milligan, had been born in the house some 75 years earlier and she drew up a shortlist of seven prospective buyers. Amazingly, she chose us to be the new owners of 32 Cassiobury Park Avenue.

'Why us?' we asked, grateful but stunned at the blessing.

'When I was showing people around and they said, "We'll alter that, knock down that wall," I thought to myself, "Oh no you won't." Whereas you liked the house just as it is and you didn't want to alter it. Plus I knew you would look after my garden.'

We knew then that this house was a gift from God, and now, with a living room packed full of hungry, homeless guys, we could see why.

Despite my initial shyness, I enjoyed hosting our evenings together and got on really well with the guys. We never knew who would turn up week on week, but there were often about 12 of us, so we would squeeze onto the sofas and sit on the floor to make space for everyone. People would say to Sheila and me, 'Aren't you afraid, having all those men in your house?' No, we were not afraid. We always tried to have John Bishop, a former Tower Club helper, around for peace of mind, but we never had any reason to fear. John was a civil servant, quiet and dignified, who enjoyed putting his faith into action in this way. We prayed before each evening and as we waited on God and read the scripture from Isaiah that he had given us, we trusted him to be our 'rear guard' and protector as we did his work.

We had a regular group of guys who came, and they treated us with respect and never caused any trouble. Just as they were not allowed to take their bottles into church, they were not allowed to bring them into the house, so the beer and cider bottles were left on the doorstep. Thankfully the neighbours never complained at the strange sight! We would watch a video, have a barbecue, or sometimes throw a candlelit dinner party with all the trimmings (except alcohol!). The dining room looked out over the garden and the guys just loved sitting in there, eating their dinner and chatting away. They were fantastic company, so amusing and cheerful. I often wondered how I would be in the same circumstances. Once I did melon for a starter – very basic, but to them it was wonderful. Most of them had never had melon in their lives.

Sheila and I loved hanging out with them. There were some sweet, gentle characters, guys who made us laugh and who wanted to chat while we wanted to listen. We had some great times sharing together, and the only time we ever got into any arguments was when it came to watching a video. Sheila and I insisted on picking the film, and that meant no swearing, violence or sex, much to the guys' disgust! Although they were often quite vocal, secretly I do not think they really minded, as they just loved coming round.

There were only a couple of times we had any trouble, one of which was when one of our regular lads invited someone else to join us. One Sunday afternoon we were having tea together in the garden and one of the guys, Paul, who had been invited by a friend, got up to go to the bathroom. He was gone a little while, but we did not think much of it until later, when Ron came and asked where his swimming trunks were. He had left them drying in the bathroom and now they had disappeared. I looked round the group until my eyes fixed on Paul. He would not meet my gaze, and looked down sheepishly at his teacup.

'If whoever has them can put them back where they found them, I would appreciate it,' I said.

Paul owned up, said 'Sorry,' and confessed he was wearing them! Of course, it was not that we begrudged them anything – the guys would regularly ask my son Craig for a pair of socks, underwear or a t-shirt, and he happily gave them, but this was different. The regular guys had a code of honour and you certainly did not steal from your friends, even something as bizarre as a pair of swimming trunks!

The other occasion was when Bob and Rick came round one afternoon. It was another lovely sunny afternoon and we had tea in the garden. Rick was addicted to pills – any pills – and had been known to buy Smarties from unscrupulous dealers, thinking they would give him a high. Although I knew this, I did not – perhaps foolishly – see the danger coming. Rick went inside and came back looking a bit embarrassed. Then he asked me what the blue pills in the cupboard were for. My heart plummeted to my feet.

'Have you taken them?' I yelled. Everyone jumped in surprise; I never raised my voice, so this must be serious.

'No,' he replied, looking decidedly guilty.

I knew shock tactics were needed to find out. 'Tell me the truth,' I said, 'because if you have, you will bleed to death. They're Warfarin, which is used to thin the blood. They're also used as rat poison.'

As fear crossed his face, he told me he had taken a handful. Moments later I bundled him into the car and raced round to the local A and E department. They immediately pumped his stomach and kept him in overnight for observation. Thankfully we got there in time and there were no lasting side effects. We praised God for being our 'rear guard'.

Our plan to keep the location of the house a secret was not very well thought through, and of course the guys soon realised where I lived and started popping round on other evenings too, and during the day. Most of the time it was fine and in they came, even when we already had friends over. If it was not convenient we would send them off with a sandwich and they would go quite happily. Ron would often raise an eyebrow as someone new turned up at the door when he was just about to sit down to dinner, and I wondered how long it would be fair to ask him to share his home like this.

On Sundays we would have a crowd of the homeless guys over for afternoon tea, which we would have in the garden when the weather was good, and then we borrowed the church minibus to take them all over to St Andrew's Church in Chorleywood. They loved the adventure of piling into the minibus and driving out into the leafy Hertfordshire countryside. The alternative was sitting in a bedsit or, worse, making a bed for the night in a skip. Most of them had no families to speak of, no one to visit or to take care of them on a Sunday.

Pete would say to me, 'This is the highlight of my week – it's such a treat to come into a nice home, have some tea, and feel like a normal person.' His face would puff up with pride as he said it and my heart ached that this simple thing was so special, as it was his closest link to normality. Pete had known family life previously, as he had a son and a daughter, but alcohol and drugs had taken their toll on his life.

45

We looked like an interesting bunch as we rolled into church, some of the party looking more respectable than others. But most of the congregation were warm and welcoming, which amazed many of the guys. Quite a few of them had never known love in their lives, and sadly had not expected to find it here. Of course, many people were not sure how to handle a large group of homeless guys in their church – most were from very comfortable middle-class backgrounds and had never met a homeless person before. I used to pray as we drove over that people would smile, say hello and not leave them standing there alone as people mingled before and after the service – for as much as the church did not know how to take them, the guys certainly did not know how to take the church members. Although the guys were usually spirited, some were intimidated and did not want to cause any trouble, offend anyone or be looked down on. They were used to being shunned: few would look them in the eye when they lived on the streets, and the smallest kindness therefore meant so much.

Most of them had never set foot inside a church like St Andrew's, which was so modern and vibrant. It was full of young people who, the guys noted, could have been down the pub instead of there every week passionately praising God. Church was also fun. The vicar at the time was David Pytches. He was a warm, loving, humble man who took time to shake the guys' hands on leaving and called them by name. That meant such a lot to them. He would also tell jokes to aid his sermon along, which was quite radical as far as the lads were concerned. David was aided and abetted by his curate Barry Kissell, and this often became a double act whereby Barry would be convulsed with laughter to the point of not being able to speak! The lads loved it. 'Who said Christianity was boring?' they were heard to say. I always felt Jesus was smiling down with approval, knowing that David and Barry were two amazing men of God who just lived to do his will.

46

Over the weeks and months we saw many give their lives to Jesus. Brian responded to a talk on 'you are a new creation'; Tom just loved Jesus and being able to worship extravagantly; Paul, Pete, Dave and many others said 'yes' to the offer of new life in Jesus. It was an exciting time, but we had little idea how to disciple these precious new converts effectively and saw little outward sign of changed lives. Some did not make a commitment but loved to come with us anyway, like Brian, who was a tiny chap, brought up by nuns who had abused him. Perhaps unsurprisingly, he was very much anti-Christianity when we met, but as he came to St Andrew's he grew to love the worship music there and to feel the love and warmth of the congregation.

Over the next few months they continued to come to our home and to church with us. We arranged for some to go to Booth House, a Salvation Army rehabilitation centre in Whitechapel, where they fought hard to come off the drink and drugs. Often, though, with no secure home and without a strong faith, the pressure was too much for them and they would fall off the wagon again.

With the guys turning up at our house on different nights and during the day, I was very thankful to have such a supportive husband who was unperturbed when he came home to find various people in his armchair or using his bathroom. Ron was working in London at the time, and one night he came home at seven o'clock after a hard day and found me in the kitchen talking to some guys and Craig hanging out and playing guitar with others in the lounge. He could not sit down and relax in his own house and I had not had a chance to make any dinner for him. Although he was not upset, I threw up a silent prayer: 'God, it's got too big. Please help!'

Steve's story

Praise be to the God and Father of our Lord Jesus Christ, the Father of compassion and the God of all comfort, who comforts us in all our troubles, so that we can comfort those in any trouble with the comfort we ourselves receive from God.
2 Corinthians 1:3–4

I used to think drinking wasn't my problem; living was. Why would I want to live? And if I had to live, why did I want to be conscious of my situation and surroundings? I was living in hell. Nothing else mattered except getting money to pay for alcohol. I had nowhere to sleep, would go for days without speaking to anyone, had lost control of my bladder and bowels and stank so much it turned my own stomach. I was considered the scum of society, kicked and spat on by passers-by. Drinking myself into oblivion wasn't a desire but a compulsion.

Children believe what their parents tell them and think that whatever happens to them is what is happening to everyone around them. For me that meant helping my alcoholic mother run a nursing home from the age of 11 and being given a bottle of sherry every Saturday night to 'teach me to respect alcohol'. My elder brother wasn't interested so I drank his share, enjoying the sweet taste that reminded me of cough mixture. The dark bottle had a mosaic pattern of a woman on it and when I'd finished it I would raid my mother's overloaded drinks cabinet and see what else I could lay my hands on. You name it, she had it, and so I tucked into a cocktail of Bacardi, vodka and gin. Anything except beer, which I hated.

My mum was too busy covering up her own drinking to worry about what I was getting up to. She was an intelligent woman who was always beautifully turned out in mink coats, huge diamonds and white gold watches that completed the façade of wealth and respectability. She had an amazing way of turning on the charm, so no one realised that she was drinking heavily to forget my father, who had died when I was five, and to help her through a messy divorce from my stepfather.

I always did well at school, speaking both German and English as my family had lived abroad, and was easily able to finish my homework in the evenings before sorting out the rotas for staff, getting their National Insurance and wages paid, and ordering stock that was needed. My mind was quick, so I had no problem picking up any jobs that needed to be done and didn't feel burdened by the work at all.

Things went horribly wrong when my mother returned from a tour of Canada when I was 16. She'd been using money from the nursing home to fund her trips and extravagant lifestyle, but couldn't understand that this was why the business wasn't making more profit. She accused me of stealing from her, and when I tried to show her the bills from her spending, she threw a fit. I'd been collecting tropical fish for five years and the walls of my room were lined with tanks hosting all kinds of the creatures. In her rage she went and pulled the fuse from the electricity that fed the tanks, to try and kill them. I retaliated and threw her Benina Swiss, the Rolls-Royce of sewing machines, down the stairs. My brother stepped in to my mum's defence and attacked me, beating me so hard I had no choice but to leave the house.

My world turned upside down. We couldn't reconcile our differences. She thought I was crazy and even sent psychiatrists round to see me, believing the problems were all mine. I stayed with friends and began to drink like a fish to cover up the pain and hurt. I thought everyone was like my mum – liars, hypocrites and thieves, able to cover it up with a good appearance. I'd taken a cleaning job on top of my studies for an OND in Tourism, and despite the drinking managed to keep them both up. I hated being drunk, but I had such an intense compulsion to keep drinking that I felt powerless to stop myself. I'd had a faith in God since I was 11, but now began to turn my back on Him in anger – how could He let this happen?

It was the beginning of a downward spiral. Although I managed to keep my jobs for many years and even got promoted to stage manager of the theatre I'd been cleaning, the drinking got worse and worse until eventually I became unemployable. I realised things had got out of hand and so I went to AA, where I found a fellowship of like-minded people who became like family to me. They taught me to put my trust back in God and to realise I was powerless against the magnetism of alcohol. With their help I stayed sober for seven years. As I pulled my life back together, I started a Psychology degree at the local polytechnic, made new friends and cut back on my AA meetings. At a party one of the other students thought it would be funny to put vodka in my drink. I could smell it from a mile off, but thought, 'It's a party and it's only one drink,' but of course after that first taste the compulsion came back as strong as ever. I kept up with my studies and nobody seemed to notice or care how much alcohol I was consuming. I was renowned for being the campus drunk, but people thought it was funny, entertained by my double backwards somersaults that I could only do when inebriated. I'd been getting Firsts in my coursework, but when it came to the exams the papers would swim in front of my drunken eyes and I couldn't concentrate. I ended up with a 2:2 degree.

I moved to Watford to be with my girlfriend Susan, and began working in a bar. Susan couldn't understand my drinking and would tell me she knew two Steves. She could tell which one had come home to her just by the look in my eye. I was unpredictable, and when she inevitably broke up with me the drinking took hold even more strongly and became a 24-hour obsession. I thought I'd tried every solution – I'd put my whole heart into believing in God and into the AA meetings, and I felt that if they couldn't help me there was no hope. I thought there was no way out for me.

I'd heard that Antibuse, a drug that made your body incapable of processing the toxins in alcohol, would make you very ill if you took one tablet and had a drink. I took a whole bottle and washed it down with a bottle of brandy, hoping it would kill me. For the next three days I was in agony, vomiting blood and sick with diarrhoea, convinced I was dying and waiting for the end. To my disgust I survived, but my landlord kicked me out because I'd made such a mess of the bedsit, and I was homeless again. In desperation I even tried to hang myself, but the cord snapped. I wondered if God was saving me for a purpose, so I began reading my Bible again and searching for a church, hoping to make some sense of why I was still alive.

No one would rent me a room, and who could blame them? I was incapable of holding down a job, and any money I got was used for alcohol, not paying the rent. Sometimes friends would let me stay, but more often than not I'd take myself down to the park, where it was quiet. I hated town and was scared of people. Homeless people were considered the lowest of the low, an easy target for people on the way home from the pub, or for bored teenagers who would think it was funny to throw water over me or kick me. My life made Groundhog Day seem like a tea party.

The days and nights rolled on in a monotonous pattern of misery, with no way out. There was a strange community among the homeless; we'd help one another out whenever we could. If you had drink and someone else didn't, you'd share yours, knowing they would do the same for you. We all understood that we couldn't live without it. Our worlds revolved around getting the money for alcohol, and nothing else seemed important.

One of the other guys told me about a couple of women called Janet and Sheila who were inviting homeless people into their homes for a meal. It sounded too good to be true. There must be some ulterior motive, I thought. I'd go round with the other lads for Sunday lunch, even in my alcoholic haze amazed that someone would treat us with such kindness and respect. Most people thought we deserved to be where we were on the streets, but Janet and Sheila showed us undying love. I was surprised by how calm they were, inviting all the maddest, most drunken men into their homes, but they seemed to know they were protected, and of course we respected their kindness.

Every now and then I'd go to church with them, but I was too committed to alcohol to find room in my life for anything else. There were days when I was lucid and purposeful. When I heard that Janet's and Sheila's charity, New Hope Trust, wanted to open a hostel, I went round all the local businesses and residents to canvas support and later helped fit out their new charity shop. But the drink was taking its toll and I was losing my sense of reality. I hallucinated frequently and would often have to reach out and touch things to see if they were real or imagined. I felt lost in a hideous nightmare.

Sometimes I couldn't stomach water until I had a few cans of strong lager inside me, and then one day I began to dry retch even the alcohol. It took me three hours to walk one mile to the doctor's, who sent me straight on to the hospital. I have no memory of how I got there. My body was so weak and the world was spinning so much that I couldn't even sit in the A and E waiting room. Most of the medical staff had no time for us drunks, but thankfully the doctor working that evening came out to see me and I was kept in while they tried to rehydrate and detox me. I refused the medication, paranoid about getting addicted to something else.

Even leaving hospital, I wasn't in a good enough state to take care of myself, but the social workers had spoken to New

Hope Trust and arranged a temporary bed for me at New Hope House. The first few weeks were a blur, but I do remember sitting and reading the Bible that Janet had given me. I was still suspicious and untrusting of people; I thought Janet had stolen the Bible, although she told me it was given to her by the Gideons!

I'd never stopped believing in God; I just thought he didn't like me, and I remember sitting and poring over Job, fascinated by this character who went through so much suffering and yet was so known and loved by the Almighty. Through the help of the workers at the shelter and my faith in God, I managed to stay sober, which is harder than coming off the drink in the first place. Having a place at the shelter was the first stability I'd had in years and meant that someone noticed and cared whether I was drinking myself into oblivion. The staff were kind, but by no means soft, and you couldn't get much past them.

After so many years of being shown no respect and feeling worthless, I was suddenly being loved and cared for. Through New Hope Trust I was also given the opportunity to meet a lot of lovely, stable people. Janet had taken me along to a local church that was full of young people who were passionate for God, and they asked me to join one of their cell groups. Still wary of strangers, it took me a while to trust them, but my leaders faithfully picked me up each week from the shelter and I felt comfortable and accepted by the group.

I had always loved hard work and persuaded the Trust to let me do some voluntary work at their day centre – the place where they gave a meal and somewhere to sit to many homeless people from the area. This gave me a window into the job market again, building my confidence and giving me experience and references which I could use to apply for other jobs.

After nine months at New Hope House I felt ready to find my own place, and the Trust helped me get a one-bedroomed flat. I kept going to church and my AA meetings and felt most alive when I was helping others who had been through similar things to me. The Bible says that God is 'the Father of compassion and the God of all comfort, who comforts us in all our troubles, so that we can comfort those in any trouble with the comfort we ourselves receive from God' (2 Corinthians 1:3-4). I know that God has brought me through so much, and I want to help others who are going through the same kind of thing.

My life has been completely transformed and is now beyond my wildest dreams. I've never wanted lots of money, or to be considered really successful. It may sound strange, but all I ever wanted was a normal life. Now I'm happily married to a wonderful nurse, I'm a self-employed builder and have been sober for more than a year. In the past, a day of being sober was beyond my comprehension, as I couldn't imagine that even a day without drink would be worth living. I received so much love and care from the people I met through the Trust, and I still work closely with other alcoholics to try and do for them what was done for me. When I thought there was nothing left for me, when I thought there was no hope for my life and no reason to go on, the faithful servants of God at New Hope Trust helped me get back on my feet and build a new life.

4: Mobile homes

The LORD will deliver them to you, and you must do to them all that I have commanded you. Be strong and courageous. Do not be afraid or terrified because of them, for the LORD your God goes with you; he will never leave you nor forsake you ... The LORD himself goes before you and will be with you ... Do not be afraid; do not be discouraged.
Deuteronomy 31:5, 8

Just a few days after throwing up that plea to God, I was in the middle of doing the ironing when the phone rang. It was Luke, one of our regulars, and from the tone of his voice I knew something was wrong. He was in hospital – a common occurrence for the homeless men with drinking problems – but this time he had got himself into trouble and the police had said that when he left hospital it was either prison or rehab. He had chosen a rehab centre about 20 miles from Watford and was phoning to ask me if I would go and visit him there. When he told me the name, Dove Word, I felt a prickle of hope for Luke's situation: it sounded as if it might be a Christian organisation.

The following week I drove to see Luke. 'You'll find it quite easily,' he had told me. 'They have two old coaches on the council car park behind Sainsbury's in the centre of High Wycombe, and a brand new day centre next door.' I found my way around the one-way system and there were the coaches, battered and worn, with clapped-out engines. Intuitively I knew that this creative use of the vehicles was the answer to my 'God, it's got too big' prayer.

Luke introduced me to Jen, the feisty Scottish lady who ran the centre. She was indeed a Christian, with a passionate love for God and a desire to show the love of Jesus to the homeless and vulnerable. At just five feet tall, her small frame belied the fact that she was a force to be reckoned with. Her black hair was pulled back into a neat bun, she was smartly dressed and she meant business. I discovered that for many years she had been working locally, initially driving around in her little Panda taking flasks of nourishing soup and warm blankets to the lads who slept in the car park and anyone else who needed them. As she had begun to realise that there was a greater need than she could cater for, she had raised local support, mainly from the churches, and invested in two coaches. The council had loaned them a site where they could leave them static and the interiors had been remodelled so that they provided a great place to serve tea, coffee and food and give people a place to sit and chat.

'If you're ever thinking of getting rid of them, would you give us first refusal?' I asked, having told her about our growing desire to help homeless people in Watford.

Jen's eyes shone as she replied, 'Now we've got a purpose-built day centre, we need to get rid of the coaches – and I've been praying about where they should go next!'

Jen loved 'her boys' to the point that she had some of them living with her and her family. She had been faithful to God and He to her, and she had worked so hard to provide this beautiful new day centre to replace the coaches. It was extravagantly and comfortably furnished, with Austrian blinds, a beautiful fitted kitchen, a large seating area and room for offices upstairs. Jen said that Roy Castle had done them the honour of cutting the ribbon on their open day.

I was stunned, but so excited. I could not wait to tell Sheila and John Bishop, who had been helping us, how God had provided so quickly. The coaches had to be moved by the end of the year, as the nearby supermarket had permission to develop the land on which they were standing. It was October already, and logic dictated that we would never find a piece of land in a town like Watford at such short notice. But we knew that this was God's plan to help the homeless, as He loved them so much more than we could, and so we felt a growing confidence that He would provide the land too.

One of the guys who had been coming to my house regularly was Chris Lloyd, a handsome and striking chap at over six feet tall, who had owned his own business but had struggled with alcohol. Chris had a council flat, but had known happier times with his wife and two children. When we told everyone about the idea of the coaches, Chris got really excited and suggested we try a site on Whippendell Road that he knew to be derelict and was just a few minutes' walk from the town centre. I went to the Town Hall to track down the owner of the land and came across the name of the builder, Peter Beckett. I phoned him and he invited me over to talk. I knew this was a significant meeting and got everyone to pray and once again thanked God that He had promised to go before me.

I drove to Pinner to Peter's office and found a tall, kindly man waiting for me. I shared our vision with him. Peter told me that he had been forced to suspend the building programme he had planned because of the high interest rates and insecure housing market at that time. He was sympathetic to our plight, particularly as he had a close relative whose life had been affected by alcohol. To my amazement, he gave me the keys there and then!

'One day I'll need the site back to build some retirement flats,' he said, 'but in the meantime you're welcome to use the land – just let me know how it goes.'

I was overjoyed, and thanked him profusely. He shook my hand when really I wanted to throw my arms around him in a huge hug. I mumbled something about drawing up a lease, and off I went, thanking God over and over again.

Sheila and I surveyed what was to be the coaches' home. Although the location was perfect, the site itself was full of rubble and semi-demolished buildings. We would need it cleared pretty quickly, but Sheila knew someone in the trade who could help us and suggested we get the homeless guys involved too. After several days' hard effort, the site was eventually cleared. Now we just needed to get the coaches themselves to the land. A friend at St Andrew's gave me the name of a commercial recovery firm who might be able to help. I spoke to the owner, Terry Williams, and my heart sank as he said it would cost £300 per coach to move them. My mind began to race. Where would we find so much money? 'However,' he continued, allowing hope to rise in me again, 'as you're Christians and this is such a good cause, I'll do it for nothing!'

The 3rd January 1990 was a fantastic day as Sheila and I stood with Irish Pat, Billy Frost, Chris Lloyd, my sister Ann and some of the others on the empty site, watching as they brought the coaches in. Spontaneous applause broke out and we all grinned from ear to ear, amazed and delighted at how God had foreseen our needs and provided so perfectly and with such good timing.

Next we had to get planning permission, which meant I spent many hours down at the local Labour party HQ and at council meetings. It felt as if I was on a fast-track training programme on how to set up a homeless drop-in centre, and I was overwhelmed by how quickly everything was happening and how much I needed to do to keep up. The verse I was given at the time was from Deuteronomy 31:8 – 'The LORD himself goes before you and will be with you' – and I clung to that promise as I stepped far out of my comfort zone. I would consider myself a naturally shy person; I do not have the 'gift of the gab' or the cheek to ask for something for nothing, and yet here I was attending council meetings, phoning strangers and asking them to help. Every time I was about to make another call or have a meeting, I asked God to make me strong and courageous. Although I did not relish the thought of all the meetings, I knew it had to be done. I was determined that we would make this happen for the lads, and knowing that God was strengthening me, I went in His name.

The guys did their part, too, and they all worked really hard to get the site ready. They even did the plumbing for the portable toilets, and although it was a bit crude it seemed to hold together. But then we had a visit from the Department of Environmental Health and they delivered the bad news: we had situated the coaches too close to the boundary wall and they would have to be moved by three feet. 'No problem,' said Tony Hall, and the guys rallied round and heaved the coaches the required distance, only to find the plumbing collapsing around them. Silently I cried out to God, 'Help! We need a plumber!'

Within minutes, Mike Canning, a plumber we knew from a local church, came on site. 'Do you need any help today, Janet? I've got a spare afternoon,' he said, oblivious to what had just gone on.

'Thank you, God! You are truly amazing,' was my first response to a mystified Mike. Again God had gone before us and made provision for our needs.

Mike got busy repairing the pipes, while the lads started to paint the coaches. We were using the Dove Word name, pleased to be linked to the fine work Jen was doing elsewhere, but the logo involved both the name and a picture of a dove. One of the men said he could do the writing, but would not want to try painting the dove for fear of messing it up. One of our supporters, Helen Venables, overheard. 'That's handy,' she said. 'I can do the painting, but not the signwriting!'

If we had been in any doubt that God was able to provide for our every need, we were given another firm assurance just a few days later. Sheila was on site with some of the lads and they were working on the landscaping. They wanted some raised flower beds and, as they discussed it, they realised they would need a huge amount of top soil for them. The guys were getting used to answered prayers and one of them, Dave, suggested asking God for what they needed.

'Great idea,' said Sheila. 'Why don't you pray?'

Dave bowed his head briefly, and in his gruff Watford accent prayed, 'God, please give us some top soil. Amen.'

They continued with their work. Five minutes later, they looked up to see a lorry filled with topsoil, stopped at the traffic lights outside the gates. Dave was there like a shot. 'Where are you going with that, mate?'

'It's all being dumped,' the lorry driver replied.

'Then can you dump it here, please?' Dave said with a grin.

As it turned out, they had three lorry loads to get rid of, ample for our needs. God had yet again increased our faith that He could supply our needs.

We noticed amazing changes in the guys over the eight weeks it took to prepare the site. They worked like Trojans, turning up at 8am ready for a hard day's graft, uncomplaining even on bitterly cold days. It was like being part of a big family, all working together for the same cause, and it gave them a real sense of ownership of the coaches.

We had nicer problems too: people were starting to just walk on site and give us money to help the homeless. Sheila had become our treasurer and I was the secretary. It always amused Sheila that she had been no good at maths at school, but she came up trumps as treasurer, recording meticulously every pound that came in and went out. Things were again growing beyond our expectations and we knew we needed some kind of formal structure.

It was at about this time that one of our regular guys, Chris Lloyd, introduced us to his GP, Tim Robson, saying we were very similar. Straight away we recognised the same values in one another and the same desire to give these guys a better future.

Tim had been brought up in a Brethren family in south-east London where being a medical missionary was seen as the highest calling of God on your life. From a young age he loved the idea of helping people physically, and at the same time taking care of their spiritual needs. As a medical student he had been happy to lead a service on the ward, but was less comfortable reaching out to the local alcoholics and homeless people with whom some of the Christian Union regularly spent time. This changed after an organised weekend that involved spending time with guys in borstal. Tim and his friends quickly learned how tough, dehumanising and demoralising life in prison was. As he got to know the guys over subsequent visits, he realised that most of them had troubled pasts and had simply made mistakes along the way. Those weekends were a key influence for Tim, challenging him to communicate his faith to people from very different backgrounds.

Having studied tropical medicine, Tim had spent some time with Tearfund, a Christian international relief agency that works around the world. He worked in a village and refugee camp in northern Thailand, giving primary care to Laotian hill tribe refugees and training tribal workers. Some patients were heavily addicted to the locally grown opium and so the centre ran an inpatient detox programme.

When he returned to England, Tim moved to Watford to be close to his church, where he met and married Julia. He took on a GP role, telling the interviewer he would be unlikely to stay more than nine months as his intention was to fly back to Thailand and continue working out there. Little did he know that 19 years later he would still be in Watford!

A number of patients visited Tim with alcohol and drug problems. This being the 1980s, there were few facilities set up to help them and they often fell by the wayside. Tim, however, was sympathetic to their plight, and once word got round that he was a good listener who took people seriously, he found himself seeing more patients with similar problems. It was one particular patient who highlighted the desperate plight of the homeless to Tim: Alan Lupton. Alan was in his mid-twenties and lived on the streets in the local town of Hemel Hempstead, after falling out with his family. He had a great sense of humour and a keen interest in railways, longing to become a guard. He was always stuffing flags into his bulging pockets. Tim's church would hold a time of worship in the local shopping area each month, and one day the church leader came across Alan begging for money. They went off for a cup of tea and a chat, which led to Alan giving his life to God.

After that he loved to go with the team into the local schools and share what God had done, warning the teenagers not to get involved with drink like he had done. With an alcoholic father, Alan had started drinking when he was about 15 and found it extremely hard to get sober. In good times he would stay with families from the church, but he would often fall off the wagon and disappear, going on drinking binges for weeks on end.

The local hospital in Watford was being rebuilt, and one of the old buildings – the empty shell of the morgue – lay empty and unused. It was Christmas-time and, with nowhere else to go, Alan broke into the morgue, planning to drink himself into oblivion. A guy from a local church heard he was there and visited him on Christmas Day, taking him turkey sandwiches and blankets and lighting some candles to combat the darkness. Tragedy struck that night. In his alcoholic stupor Alan fell asleep too close to the candles; his clothes caught fire and he was unable to rouse himself enough to get away.

Tim was on his way to visit relatives when he took a phone call on Boxing Day telling him what had happened. He was devastated that Alan's life had ended in such a way, and as the crowd gathered for Alan's funeral he felt a growing sense that it should never be allowed to happen again. Although Tim was able to provide some help as a GP, he knew that more needed to be done – he just did not know what. When Chris Lloyd told Tim about the work we were beginning to do with the coaches, Tim was keen to meet us, and he soon realised that this would be the vehicle to give the help that was so desperately needed.

Sheila and I immediately asked Tim to be our chairman, knowing that as an articulate and passionate doctor with a warm heart and a love for God and for the homeless, he would make a great ambassador for our work. Still conscious of the fact that we were just two untrained housewives, we knew that as a GP he would also add credibility to the work we were doing and help us get the right help for those who needed it.

The 23rd March 1990 dawned clear and bright, the perfect day for our official launch. We had asked Tim to lead our service of dedication along with John Woodger (our vicar) and Father Scholes from the local Catholic church. We were as excited as children at Christmas, thrilled to be able to tell everyone what God had done, proud to show off the guys' hard work in getting the site ready and eager to open so that anyone who was homeless could come and have something to eat and drink. The site looked fantastic – unrecognisable from the day we had been given the keys. The coaches stood proudly in the centre with tables and chairs outside, lined by beautiful flowers, making the whole area welcoming and inviting. More than 100 people came along as the Mayor of Watford officially opened the site, while a church group played worship songs to glorify God.

The opening service felt like a dedication to Alan Lupton and to all the other homeless men who had died over the years in our town. Now we were hoping that this provision would make such tragedies a thing of the past.

5: Provision from St Michael

*How good and pleasant it is
when God's people live together in unity!*
Psalm 133:1

One of the greatest things about the coaches was that their informal style set the tone for a relaxed and welcoming environment. People who found the cold concrete buildings of social services intimidating felt happy to walk on site and come in for a cup of tea and a chat.

The coaches themselves had been completely refitted for us. One boasted a new counter and hob where we could heat and serve soup, tea and coffee. Benches lined both coaches so that 16 people could comfortably sit, eat, drink and talk. Local churches had heard about what we were doing through articles in the local paper and by word of mouth, and we had around a dozen volunteers to start our rota, all passionate about Jesus and keen to get involved and help where they could. It has been such a blessing to us that the work has been cross-denominational. The churches have been unified in working together to help the homeless, putting aside differences and allowing their aim to be the same: to show the love of Jesus in a practical way.

Those first months were so busy that we felt as if we were constantly on the go. The coaches were open every day and Sheila, Tim and I would meet regularly together at 6.30am to pray and offer the day to God. If it sounds as if we were amazing prayer warriors; let me set you straight: there was just no other time we could all get together! We were so busy, but we did not want to make the fatal mistake of being too busy to ensure that God was at the centre of all we did. We were always aware that, although God wanted us to reach out practically and provide food and comfort, the guys needed so much more than we could give. God called us to trust Him, to seek Him and to ask Him to pour out His Holy Spirit on them, so that we might see their lives truly changed.

Sheila or I would juggle the various responsibilities in our lives so that one of us could arrive at 9am to pray and set everything up ready to open at 10.00. The guys would already be waiting at the gates. With nowhere else to go, they simply stood on the streets waiting until we could get a cup of tea ready for them. We contacted our local bakers, Marks and Spencer and Boots stores and they happily agreed to give us all their leftover sandwiches. Sheila would go to pick up the sandwiches every evening and then get them to the coaches the following morning before taking her grandson Ben to school. She would often tell me later that she had gone to get extra food the night before, 'just in case there weren't enough leftovers for our needs'. She always laughed to herself when she then collected the goods and there was so much more than we could use! Although we feared not having enough food each day, we were learning as we went along that God would provide for us, and He never let us down. In fact, once they were aware of our work, local businesses donated so much food that at one point Sheila had two extra fridges and a freezer in her back garden to be able to store all the fresh produce we were given!

When we opened the gates, the guys would troop in hungry and cold, ready to wolf down the tea, coffee, hot chocolate, cakes and biscuits. We would make the tea, get the soup and sandwiches ready for lunch, or just sit and chat, getting to know the guys, with Christian music playing unobtrusively in the background. With much of the lunch coming from Marks and Spencer, it was great seeing the guys tuck into such good-quality food – although they often picked their way through the smoked salmon sandwiches hunting for a regular cheese and ham one!

People at local churches said they would like to help but did not know how much they could actually do. Many of them had never really spoken to a homeless person before, so it was natural that they were hesitant, worried they would find themselves out of their depth and tongue-tied, or afraid they would upset the guys by saying the wrong thing. 'There's nothing to it!' we would reassure them. 'Just come along and say hello. You can make the tea or just sit with someone. You don't need any special skills, and one of their greatest needs is just for someone to say hi and treat them like anyone else. They often don't get to talk to anyone.'

The homeless men told us that feeling ostracised and overlooked by people as they walked past was one of the hardest things about living on the streets. They valued the support that the volunteers gave them, even if it was just asking how they were. So volunteers soon settled in and relaxed, realising that there was no magic secret – just the ability to make a cuppa and have a chat!

After we had said goodbye each afternoon, we would clear up before heading off to collect the food for the next day. Then Sheila would go home and make soup for the following day, usually aided and abetted by one of the lads, Dave, who was happy to lend a hand chopping vegetables.

Often Sheila would be at the coaches while I was out and about talking to people about what we were doing, raising support and money. Our initial running costs were only about £120 a week and the local churches were keen to help. I set up a makeshift office in my spare room and when I was not at the coaches with Sheila, I would be working on the administration that went with our work. They were natural roles for us and we found we fitted into them easily, each playing to our strengths.

When we started we had about 20 guys coming each day, some wanting just to have some food and head off again; others enjoying the company and staying all day. Every Tuesday we ran a Bible study, as we were keen to make it clear that this was God's provision for the homeless. Most of them were really open to hearing about God, and about half a dozen of them regularly came along. Others, like Brian who came on site and introduced himself with the words, 'Don't you dare talk to me about Christianity!' were not so keen. Either way, we offered food and fellowship. While making our faith clear, we also made sure no obligation or pressure was put on anyone to become a Christian.

That summer we even took a group from the coaches down to the Christian conference New Wine, where they worked as stewards. They loved being a part of everything, being given walkie-talkies, taking their responsibilities seriously and donning their smart yellow jackets with pride. It was an amazing privilege for us to see them worship and praise God too. Tommy was so in love with Jesus that the chief steward had to keep tapping him on the shoulder in the main meetings and reminding him that he also had duties to do while praising his heart out!

While those early days were great fun and so exciting, we were on a steep learning curve at the coaches and encountered a number of problems. When we were given donations we would use them to put down deposits for bedsits. We found some sympathetic landlords and, while the rooms were basic, they were a much safer prospect than the streets. People would give us furniture, so the guys would have a bed to sleep in and a chair to sit on, and we spent many hours collecting and transferring everything. Sheila and I decided to pool some of our own money to invest in a minibus. This meant that the guys could drive it too and we did not always have to be around if things needed moving. Most of the time this was fine, but on one occasion we discovered that one of the lads had in fact been selling the goods on rather than taking them to their intended homes! We were sad and disappointed that our trust had been abused, and we said he could not drive the bus again. But for the most part the guys relished responsibility of any sort – feeling a sense of ownership in the work and satisfied that there were things they could do to help.

One of our volunteers, Mary, was getting closer to some of the men and began to go to their bedsits to do Bible studies. We told her we did not think it was appropriate, as she was married, but she said that she and her husband were both fine with the situation. She carried on against our wishes, growing particularly close to a guy called Andrew. We tried to do the right thing, first speaking to Mary on her own, then to her husband and then to her vicar. We did all we could, but she was quite unrepentant. It was not long before we heard that she had left her husband to be with Andrew and had taken the children with her.

It was a hard time for us all. We did not think it appropriate that she should come on site with Andrew any more, but the lads did not understand. We were learning as we went; there was no volunteer support, no proper policies and procedures in place, and we were certainly no experts.

We did not have much trouble from the guys, though. It helped that we had mainly female volunteers, as the lads respected them and would try not to swear in front of them, let alone fight. All the men who had been involved felt such a sense of ownership and pride in the coaches that they were not about to let anyone spoil them or take advantage of us. There was a real family spirit and sense of community, and if anyone new came on site and started to cause trouble, the regulars would look after us and see them off.

The word began to spread among the homeless, and social services, local GPs and the police heard about what we were doing and referred people to us, so gradually our numbers grew. By the end of the first year we had about 80 people visiting the coaches each day, including a growing number of women. It was not just the homeless any more: people who were unemployed or living in bedsits, or single parents struggling to bring up their kids, would all come for the food and the company on offer. Often it just provided a much-needed structure to their days. When the weather was fine it was OK, as we could sit outside and the kids had somewhere to play, but on rainy days we began to realise that we needed more space as we all squashed inside the coaches.

One of our supporters worked for Laings and he asked his boss to give us a Portakabin, which meant we had more space and could do some one-on-one work, helping people with their numeracy and literacy. It also doubled as a good games room, and many an afternoon was spent playing one of the multitude of board games that had been donated. Jennifer Ashdown made the Portakabin as homely as possible with vases of flowers, and she would encourage the guys and girls to display their artwork on the walls. She had seen God's miraculous power first hand when he had healed her mother's blindness a few years earlier, and she knew what a difference He could make to people's lives. She shone with the radiance of Jesus and we loved having her as part of the team.

Someone had given us a beautiful wall clock, which we mounted proudly above the door. One day I looked up at the place where it normally was, and it was gone. I asked Jennifer and she paled. 'Someone must have taken it,' she said quietly.

I was shocked and started to get angry. 'After all we've done for them, this is how they repay us!' I thought indignantly. Out loud, I said to Jennifer, 'How could they do this to us when we've given them everything we possibly can?'

She shrugged her shoulders and said, 'Let's pray and ask God to bless them – and you never know, God may bring it back.' I do not think we ever saw that clock again, or found out who had taken it, but I was truly humbled by her gracious attitude.

As word got round about what we were doing, we had more people donate clothes and we set up a caravan next to the coaches to hold them all. The guys would go in there and see one of our volunteers, Pat, who would find clothes that fitted. As she got to know them she would hang on to pieces as they came in, knowing who they would be right for. They loved her and grew to trust her. Often someone would go in for a new jumper and stay for an hour while they told Pat about the pain in their lives, and Pat would share with them about Jesus.

There were, however, a growing number of needs for which we were not able to cater. Some were solved practically by linking up with the council. For example, we wanted to provide somewhere for people to wash, but we had no showers. We worked out an arrangement with the local swimming baths, who let us use their facilities, and that was one more service we could get access to for our regulars.

Other problems were not so easily solved. More people were coming on site with mental health problems and we would do our best to help them remember to take their medication. Many were addicted to drugs and alcohol; some were ill and desperately needed a place to stay. We knew that if they did not have a home, they could not get a job, and without a job it was almost impossible to get a home. We found it so hard to shut the doors at 3pm every day, knowing that the people had nowhere else to go, not knowing if they would be safe. The coaches were great for meeting the short-term need for food and somewhere to be in the day, and for providing some fellowship and support, but the hunger was growing in us to do more. As winter approached, the needs grew even stronger: it was predicted that the temperature would regularly drop below zero at night, and we knew that many of those we had come to know as friends might not make it through to spring if they were living on the streets in the freezing cold.

We had to do something.

6: New Hope for a winter of discontent

'For I know the plans I have for you,' declares the LORD, 'plans to prosper you and not to harm you, plans to give you hope and a future.'
Jeremiah 29:11

That first winter after we opened the coaches was as cold as predicted. As the temperature dropped and the snow began to fall thick and fast, we upped our efforts to provide a night shelter. There was no time or money to provide a house with beds, so we got in touch with the council, who through emergency powers were able to let us use the multiracial centre right in the middle of town.

The centre was used in the evenings for things like judo classes, and when they had finished, usually by about 10pm, the centre became ours. A hospital that was closing gave us lots of old mattresses and we spread them out on the hall floor, gathering as many warm blankets and duvets as we could find to make the guys as comfortable as possible. We would give them a warm meal when they arrived and, although the sleeping arrangements were very basic, it was at least shelter from the freezing temperatures.

The great thing about it being such an informal arrangement was that anyone who turned up and needed somewhere to stay could just grab an extra mattress and bed down – there was flexibility on the number of people who could sleep there. Some came back every night; others just for a couple – like Jeff, a smart businessman who had owned his own home and found himself homeless after his business went down the drain during the recession and his marriage collapsed. He came just for a few nights and was able to pick himself up and get back to normal life quite quickly. We did not have much trouble –

although some of the lads sent us out to buy earplugs as they could not stand the sound of the other men snoring!

We had no money to pay staff to work there, so different churches in the area took responsibility for each night, and Sheila and I were there every evening to make sure everyone settled down OK. The centre had to be cleared by 8am so we arranged with a local café for the guys to go and get coffee and toast in the morning, which gave them somewhere warm to be before we opened the coaches again. It also gave us a short window of opportunity to swab all the mattresses with disinfectant and take all the blankets to the dry cleaners so they would be ready again for the next night.

As December rolled on, we began to make plans for our first Christmas Day together. We wanted to give our homeless friends everything that so many families would be sitting down to that day – a full roast with all the trimmings – but we only had a hob at the coaches and no oven. So we each brought our microwaves from home and split the food: I did the potatoes and vegetables and Sheila did the turkey and bacon-wrapped sausages. Sheila's experience as head cook at a school came in very useful and I was glad to have her organising everything in her efficient way! Forty people arrived, but she took the catering all in her stride and served up each plate with a cheerful 'Merry Christmas!' and a smile, and she had a great team of helpers who plated up the food and heated it all through as each person arrived.

The table was beautifully decorated; tinsel and baubles decked out the Portakabin and made it look festive. It was a real family Christmas – Ron and Craig came with me and Sheila brought her grandson Ben, and we enjoyed the amazing blessing of being surrounded by so many of the men and women we had come to call friends over the previous year. It felt so right to share such a special holiday with them.

After the Christmas puddings we had tea and coffee and then began to open gifts. Local churches and schools had donated presents, and after lunch Sheila took on the role of Santa – sitting with a box of women's gifts on one side, a box of men's on the other, and a huge sack for the kids to dip their hands into and pull out a toy right in front of her. Everyone was happy. Most of the people who came were in disbelief that so much had been laid on for them – the mums particularly, who knew they would not have been able to provide such food and presents for their kids, were overwhelmed with gratitude. Mainly it was our regular group, but there was one guy – Matt – who was deaf and dumb and had nowhere else to be on that day. Social services told him we were opening and he came to join us. Every year after that he came back, and even though we never saw him during the rest of the year, it was like catching up with a relative you only see at Christmas and we were glad to have him with us.

We felt truly blessed to have been part of such a special day and were so thankful to all the people who had donated the food and presents to make it happen. We played games long into the afternoon. The following day, while I went to visit family, Sheila cooked up bubble and squeak for anyone who wanted it and opened the coaches for a Boxing Day gathering.

Although we greatly admired the work Jen was doing with Dove Word Ministries, it was around the start of 1991 when Sheila, Tim and I began to feel sure that we should set up our own Watford-based charity, independent of Dove Word but with strict accountability measures. So after consulting various people, we became a separate charity. I had read and been impacted by a passage in 2 Chronicles 7:14, 19–21 which said,

> If my people, who are called by my name, will humble
> themselves and pray and seek my face and turn from
> their wicked ways, then will I hear from heaven, and I
> will forgive their sin and will heal their land … But if

you turn away and forsake the decrees and commands I have given you … then I will … reject this temple which I have consecrated for my Name. I will make it a byword and an object of ridicule among all peoples. This temple will become a heap of rubble. All who pass by will be appalled.

We found out a few years later that Dove Word was being closed by the Charity Commission because of improprieties. We were deeply saddened, as the closure resulted in many people being disillusioned and it was a great blow for those whom Jen had served so faithfully. The words from Chronicles came back to us. Dove Word's new day centre had previously been an imposing thing of beauty, but somehow it had all gone horribly wrong. It reminded us again that we were not above falling; we had to stick closely to God and humble ourselves in prayer regularly.

Now that we were a new charity we needed a new name, so Sheila, Tim and I all went off to pray. When we met up to discuss some possible ideas, we realised we were all thinking along the same lines: hope. We had all read the scripture from Jeremiah 29:11 in which God promises that He has plans to give us 'hope and a future', and we felt this was a really important part of what we wanted to offer anyone with whom we worked. We became Watford New Hope Trust – feeling that 'New' added strength to the title and conveyed the message we wanted to get across.

While we were aware that we were only weak, we knew that God was strong, and with Him there is always hope for everyone. It was humbling for us to be involved in what God was doing and we loved seeing Him at work in people's lives – people like Eddie Barrs, who came shuffling onto the coach one morning wearing a big beige camel-hair coat and with little tufts of hair sticking out in all directions from his head. He had a bag over one shoulder which he clutched to him and did not put down all day. We made him a drink and asked him where he came from. To our surprise, he said he had walked all the way from a town almost ten miles away. He lived in a flat there – but to be completely honest, he was so messy and smelly that we had thought he lived in a skip. One of the volunteers offered to give him a lift home when we closed, as it was so far for him to walk, and they told us the next day that the flat may as well have been a skip, for all the empty cans, mouldy food, rubbish and newspaper that was strewn around. They saw his mattress out on the balcony and asked why he slept outside. 'I'm scared of the dark,' he replied, 'and there's no electricity inside, so I'd rather be out there where I can see the street lamps.'

When we heard this, we asked some of the lads to help us and one day we went over and helped him clean his flat up. It took hours to clear away all the accumulated rubbish, but it was definitely worth it. We helped Eddie clean himself up too. One of the girls who came to help out at the coaches was a hairdresser and she tidied up his tufts and deloused him while we got him new clothes. We could rarely get him to put his precious bag down, though – he held it close, tucking yoghurts and sandwiches in there for later. Every now and then one of us would manage to prise it from him and clean it out – uncovering all sorts of moulding items squashed in its depths. He always had a runny nose, too, and we spent most of our time with him getting clean tissues. He had just been released from the mental institution he had been in since he was a young boy, and we soon realised he was not capable of looking after himself.

One time when we were chatting, we got talking about holidays and he said he had never had one. We asked where he would like to go and he said Bournemouth, as he would like to see the sea. When I offered to arrange a few days away, Eddie was overjoyed. We found a friendly B&B landlady through the

Mothers' Union magazine, and when we explained Eddie's situation she said she would be happy to look after him. So one of our guys, Tommy, and I drove Eddie off for a few days by the sea.

We got a phone call from the landlady a few days later saying there was a problem. She had forgotten it was the Conservative Party conference and so she had lots of guests that week. They could not handle seeing Eddie sitting at breakfast, eating with his fingers and letting food fall down his top without wiping it up. She asked if I would come and get him, so Tommy and I drove down early one morning to collect him. Eddie had not yet ventured as far as the sea, so we took him for a big breakfast on the seafront and watched as he happily tucked into bacon and eggs while the waves crashed and rolled before us. Afterwards we walked along the beach together and took a photo of us all outside the Grand Hotel. We went home that night and Eddie said those had been the best few days of his life. His eyes shone and he talked about the wonderful time he'd had for a long time afterwards.

When we returned, we made some phone calls and eventually managed to get him into Margaret House, a local nursing home. When he was settled, he would come and visit us still and would pull out a sparkling white handkerchief. Sheila always said the sight of that hanky was enough to make her smile, as she knew it meant that someone was taking care of Eddie. We also managed to make contact with his brother, to whom Eddie had not spoken in 30 years, and they began to meet up regularly. Eddie is one of the characters who stands out in our minds even many years later. He was a lovely man who had suffered terribly from mental health problems that were not his fault, and we were so thankful that we had the privilege of meeting him. He was one of the many we consider to be the angels about whom the writer of Hebrews talks:

Do not neglect to show hospitality to strangers, for by doing that some have entertained angels without knowing it.

Hebrews 13:2 (NRSVA)

7: The keys of the kingdom

The Spirit of the Sovereign LORD is on me,
because the LORD has anointed me
to preach good news to the poor.
He has sent me to bind up the broken-hearted,
to proclaim freedom for the captives
and release from darkness for the prisoners.
Isaiah 61:1

By the second Christmas we had around 100 visitors a day to the coaches and were once again able to provide mattresses on the floor of a nearby church hall at night. Sheila and I were exhausting ourselves. Days were spent at the coaches, fundraising or undertaking the administration, and then we spent the nights helping out at the shelter. When we were tired it was hard to have grace for the guys if they grumbled and moaned. It felt as if we were giving so much, and in truth we were becoming exhausted. We decided the best thing to do was to apply for funding from Shelter Winter Watch for our first paid member of staff to come and run the night shelter. It was such a relief for us to know that anyone who came would be well looked after and we could get a much-needed break. Initially we employed Jona and Mark, both streetwise men who had overcome their own addictions and oozed the love and compassion of Jesus.

We began to dream about getting a house where the guys could stay and really rebuild their lives. Life on the streets offers no security or safety and little support, so if things were ever to change we knew we needed to provide them with a more secure and stable base. It seemed like a slightly crazy idea at first. We had managed to cover our modest outgoings so far and God had so faithfully provided for all our needs, but a house would be a huge step. We had good contacts within local churches and many more were aware of New Hope Trust through the press coverage we had received, so we wrote to them all outlining our vision for a more permanent hostel. I typed out a letter at home on my old Amstrad word processor and we mailed 100 copies to churches and local contacts, enclosing an envelope for them to return any gifts and donations. Every opportunity Tim and I had, we went and spoke to local church groups, schools, church leaders and women's groups, telling them about the great needs in Watford and what we hoped to be able to do. There was cross-political-party support as well as interdenominational church backing, and the money began to roll in.

We launched the appeal over a weekend and were completely astounded when we raised £100,000 in just a few days! We could not believe it and realised it was far beyond our capabilities as a small trust to deal with this kind of money. God had once again answered our prayers in the most amazing way. It seemed that there were many in the area who were aware of the problems of homelessness and who were keen to do something about it. Until now they had not had the chance, but New Hope Trust gave them the opportunity to make a big difference. We even had one envelope containing £1,000 in cash pushed anonymously through our door, and we never had a clue who gave it.

It is amazing how God used so many people to achieve His purposes, and He always introduced them to us at just the right time. Sheila was friends with the local Salvation Army major, Deirdre, who was a warm and lovely woman with a real heart for what we were doing. She suggested we contact the Salvation Army Housing Association (SAHA), which we did. By that time we had identified a building just round the corner from the local police station, which we thought could be handy if there was any trouble! It was a bit like a rabbit warren with so many rooms and corridors, but it was a former guest house so we thought planning permission would be quite straightforward.

SAHA were intrigued by the idea of a soup kitchen run in two old coaches that attracted volunteers from so many local churches, and they agreed to come and see us. We met Bob (the south-east development officer) and Nigel (their finance officer) at the house to give them a tour of the rabbit warren. Inevitably we all got lost and they worried about how on earth we would supervise the people living there. Unenthusiastic about the building, they still agreed to come and have a look at the coaches – and then they were bowled over! As we arrived, some 40 men and women were enjoying lunch and they happily told the visitors about the coaches and their own lives. As I saw Bob so at ease, chatting in such a warm and non-threatening manner, I recognised a kindred spirit with the same passion to help the homeless. SAHA had never worked with another organisation except the Salvation Army, but they left saying they would take the proposal of working in partnership to their chief executive and committee and suggested we keep looking for a suitable shelter.

So much had happened in that first year. We had one volunteer, Mark, who would get frustrated when some of the more able youngsters would just sit around drinking coffee all day. He had a passion to get them back to doing some form of work, so we applied for a grant from the Herts Community Trust which meant we could pay Mark a small retainer. His vision and enthusiasm inspired the guys: he secured an allotment from Watford Council for them to grow vegetables on and they painted the local Scout hut, finding purpose and fulfilment in a good day's work.

We found another house that we thought would be perfect for our needs, with a wonderful garden and a flat at the top of the building just right for Mark to live on site. We excitedly shared all the details with Bob, who gave us the go-ahead, only for us to be let down at the last moment when the owner pulled out of the sale. We were devastated. As we shared with the lads that it was not going to happen, one of them, Steve, surprised me in his response. He had come to the coaches when his life and marriage were in ruins and he had met with Jesus, giving his life over to his Saviour. That day he told me firmly, 'Janet, if God takes away something that is good; it's because He has got something better.' It was wonderful to be reminded of this truth, and how right he was! A few weeks later we were contacted by the council, who told us that the local Baptist chapel and manse were up for sale. Our hearts leaped: could this be the 'something better' that Steve had so unknowingly prophesied?

The owners of the Baptist chapel had a covenant on the building and wanted it to continue to be used as a place of worship. They looked favourably on our application as we would dedicate the building to God and it would be used in a practical outworking of Christian love and worship of God. There was some local opposition: people were wary of the idea, thinking it would increase the number of drunks and drug users in the area, and one guy even got up a petition. There was a lot of work to do in terms of persuading them that we would be closely monitoring those staying and would make sure everything would be OK. We held open meetings to reassure the local community that there would be no danger to their children or their environment, but it was not enough to persuade everyone. I well remember walking up one side of the road on which the chapel was situated, trying to allay the fears of the local shopkeepers, only to find a man walking along on the other side spreading fear and anxiety, getting folk to sign his petition of opposition. As I spoke to one shopkeeper, he greeted me with the words, 'You haven't got a hope in hell of this going through.' I felt stunned and upset and cried out to God to help us.

I carried on up the road and saw Stan, a local shopkeeper who was much more supportive. He made me a cup of tea, and to my delight there was a lad called Nigel whom I had met at one of the open meetings. He reminded me that 'if God was for it, who could be against it?' Encouraged, I opened my Bible and read these words from Psalm 132:13:

> For the LORD has chosen Zion,
> he has desired it for his dwelling.

How my heart leaped. The chapel was called Mount Zion! My faith was stirred and I praised God that He had chosen that building for his purposes, and I knew we had nothing to fear.

Over time the links with the Salvation Army proved useful in boosting our credibility, and the local people were eventually reassured. We had asked one of the local shop owners if we could use a unit near the house as a charity shop, but he turned us down. We were disappointed, but left it with God, knowing that He could so easily change the owner's mind or find us alternative premises.

What a glorious day it was when we got the keys to Mount Zion! We invited all our supporters to join us in a time of thanksgiving and celebration, and it was wonderful to see that God had indeed had something better in mind than the original building. The Rev John Woodger from St Mary's led us in singing 'To God be the glory – great things he has done', and we praised God for His goodness. We renamed the chapel New Hope House and knew without doubt that we could trust God to complete the work He had started.

While the architects worked on the plans to put in a new floor and turn the chapel into private rooms upstairs and communal areas below, we carried on providing mattresses on the floor of the church as an interim solution. Despite raising so much money, we still needed more for the sale and to help fund the conversion, so the Salvation Army Housing Association applied to the Housing Corporation and the borough council gave us £50,000. We continued fundraising, applying to charitable trusts and looking to our supporters to meet the need in order to raise enough money to furnish the building with all the necessary beds, sofas and kitchen equipment. While it was incredibly important that we did not waste money and were good stewards of everything that had been entrusted to us, we wanted to make sure that the place was not furnished shabbily. The men were more than used to 'making do' with where they slept, what they ate and what they wore, and their sense of self-worth was usually at rock bottom. We wanted them to feel a sense of pride in the place where they lived and to know something of how God valued them through the things that we provided, so we carefully picked out everything from the curtains to the bed linen and crockery.

The whole process was another steep learning curve for me. While it was easy enough to choose the soft furnishings, there were many more demanding duties to be performed. I took on the role of project manager as Tim was busy at his GP practice and Sheila continued to man the coaches. It was partly out of necessity and partly because I wanted to be heavily involved as I was so excited about the whole thing. Over the months it meant seemingly endless phone calls and meetings with builders about problems and hiccups with which anyone who has undertaken building work will be familiar. It was exhausting, but we loved going into the building each week and seeing the progress, knowing that we would finally have somewhere to offer the guys a chance to rebuild their lives.

We could not wait to dedicate the building to God, and in June 1993 we held a thanksgiving service in the chapel while the building work was still in progress. We invited everyone who had prayed, given and supported us in making it happen, offering them a chance to look round the building and see the plans. We held an open house every day for two weeks, to give everyone who had contributed to this wonderful home for the homeless a chance to see how their money had been spent.

When the work was finally finished Sheila, Tim and I were so excited to get in and see it. We wanted to look round each of the ten bedrooms, admire each freshly painted wall, each newly laid piece of carpet, the relaxing lounge, the fully equipped kitchen. Our desire was that it should feel like a home rather than a hostel, and it really did. All the while the building work had been going on we had been dreaming about how we wanted the house to run. Up until this point all the work of the Trust had relied on volunteers, but we knew it was important for the guys staying at the house to have people working with them who were committed and experienced in helping people with problems like theirs. We began recruiting a team who would manage the house, be there overnight with the residents and act as support workers for each person who stayed.

The first priority was to take care of the practical needs of those who came. Jesus gave us the example when he fed the 5,000 that he is not only interested in spiritual needs, but also cares about the everyday details of our lives. Through the coaches we had seen men whose bodies were wrecked from lack of nutrition, the abuse of alcohol or drugs, the effects of being out in all weathers and sleep deprivation, so we wanted New Hope House to be a place where we could look after them physically.

As with the coaches, we wanted to make it clear that we were Christians and to give the guys every opportunity to know God's great love and mercy for themselves. Of course, as with the coaches, our support was never conditional or reliant on them choosing Jesus, and New Hope House was to be an accepting environment for all. We decided to run Bible studies every morning and the men were free to join the team or to do their own thing. When guys came to the team with problems, we wanted the workers to offer to pray with or for them, but never to insist on it or make anyone uncomfortable.

Those who have lived on the streets have lived a very strange existence, with no discipline, no order or structure to their days and no support networks – in fact, with few of the things we take for granted. Over the years since it opened, New Hope House has been a place where they can be in a more normal home environment, participate in cleaning duties, take responsibility for going with a worker to do the weekly food shop and cook meals to help them learn to take care of themselves, and prepare for having their own place in the future. Being so involved gives the guys a sense of ownership, too, and is often the first responsibility with which they have been entrusted in a long time. Even sitting down to an evening meal together was something many of the men had not experienced for years, but we felt it would be an important element in making the house feel like a family home.

One of the major factors we needed to offer was consistency. Often the only thing that has been consistent in their lives is that people have let them down or turned their back on them (often with good reason when addiction has taken over and they will do anything to feed it). We had to make sure that staff would be unwavering in their commitment to see these men return to normal life, that they would walk the line between tough love and mercy, seeking God for how best to handle situations that would lead to the residents' growth.

The hostel is a 'dry' house, so no alcohol or drugs are permitted on site and residents are not permitted to return to the house drunk or under the influence of drugs. Each resident with a drink or drugs problem is asked to commit to a rehabilitation programme with a local group to give them the best chance of recovery and breaking free from their addiction.

We know that we have many limitations in what we offer and readily network with outside agencies and organisations such as Alcoholics Anonymous and Narcotics Anonymous.

At the time of New Hope House's opening our trustee base had increased and we were put in touch with Gordon Holloway. Former chief executive of the Shaftsbury Society, a Christian charity for men and women who are homeless or have learning difficulties, Gordon had also been an established and successful businessman. He came to us with a wealth of experience and was invaluable as we interviewed prospective candidates for the posts of project workers and manager. Sheila and I were again way out of our depth, but with Tim and Gordon we interviewed and prayed carefully. It was one of our great passions to see people who have been through difficult situations helping others who are going through the same. Two of our night wardens in those early days had previously been enslaved to addictions and were brilliantly placed to help some of our guys get clean. It was wonderful to see in practice the words from 2 Corinthians 1:4 that God 'comforts us in all our troubles, so that we can comfort those in any trouble with the comfort we ourselves receive from God'.

Our first resident moved into New Hope House in August 1993. He had just been divorced for the third time and his life had fallen apart through the misuse of drugs. He made a commitment to Christ and stayed with us for several months, but drugs are a cruel master and he succumbed once again and chose to leave. However, over the years he has been able to hold down a job and still has faith in God. Although we were not able to help him be fully freed from his addictions, New Hope was a lifeline in his time of need and played a part in his recovery.

We have had many referrals from the probation service and prisons, self-referrals when people have turned up, bag in hand, desperate for a place to sleep, or people who have been recommended through other elements of the Trust's work. While it is vital to get as clear a picture as possible of a potential client's past, our policy has always been to look to their future. This has sometimes meant turning people away for the simple and sad reason that they are not willing to change. One of the most important elements in anyone's rehabilitation is their own willingness to deal with the issues and their own desire to see their life turned round. We cannot provide that for them – we can only give them the tools, the encouragement and the environment to change. No matter how 'high risk' a resident is deemed to be, if they are willing to try, then we will give them an opportunity to do so. Because their rehabilitation is not under the control of the staff or volunteers at New Hope House, everyone has to remember to entrust to God each person with whom we come into contact and not take full responsibility for them themselves. There have been many who have stayed at New Hope House over the years, some coming to know Jesus, some not, some being freed from their addictions and going on to lead full lives, others finding the hold of alcohol or drugs too strong and leaving the home to continue their abuse. Often we have found ourselves plagued with worries over a particular person. Each time we have had to hand that over to God and ask Him to take control, knowing that He has the power to change lives and we do not.

We try to be flexible about how long residents can stay at New Hope House, as rehabilitation varies from person to person. Each individual is allocated a key worker who is responsible for helping and supporting that resident day by day. They undertake an in-depth assessment of that person's situation and work together to set achievable and stretching goals to allow for growth. They also work on the resident's behalf with other services as needed, such as the benefits agency, mental health services, job centres and training centres. All residents are encouraged to undertake voluntary work either within the Trust or with other local initiatives as a way of gaining confidence, giving back to the community and getting used to working and taking responsibility again. We now have a personal development coordinator who works at New Hope House teaching nutrition, food hygiene, shopping and cooking, all of which is documented to provide evidence of the residents' skills when they move on from the house.

We have loved seeing how our volunteers and staff make a huge difference in the lives of those staying at New Hope House. Rod Frampton and his wife Rene had come along to an open day and had loved what they saw, pledging their support for the future. Sadly Rene died shortly afterwards, but even in his grief Rod remembered the pledge they had made and volunteered his time to visit the hostel each week. He took Bible studies and became a mentor to the lads, committed to meeting with them each week and discipling them. One of the men with whom he got involved was Mike, who had a terrible drink problem.

Previously Mike had been a member of an orchestra in London, such was his talent, but sadly his life was in ruins. I had met him wandering up the road and spoke to him, suggesting that he try and get a place at the hostel. He later told me that his stay at New Hope House was the time when he discovered God's grace. Mike had been an alcoholic for years before giving his life to Jesus and found that his faith was not enough to keep him from drinking. Desperately trying to find the strength to quit, Mike stayed at a number of rehabilitation centres. His treatment was unsuccessful and he realised he was powerless when it came to alcohol. When I met him on the street he had nowhere left to turn and had become completely dependent on God to help him with his addiction. It was a great joy for us to see the transformation in Mike's life. Throughout his stay at New Hope House, he would thank God daily and constantly commit himself to God's will. Now he is no longer enslaved to his alcoholism, has his own place, again plays double bass in an orchestra and teaches many pupils privately. Although we were able to provide the bed and a base for Mike, it was Rod's faithful commitment to meeting up with him that helped Mike commit his life so fully to God. This is a constant reminder to us of the extraordinary difference our volunteers can make in people's lives.

By the time New Hope House was officially opened by the Bishop of St Albans a few months after completion, all the beds were taken and we already had a list of people waiting to come in when space became available. There were about 100 people who joined with us to thank God for the house, including everyone who had made it happen, and the local mayor, a local bishop, support agencies and our volunteers. People were crammed into the entrance hall and all the way up the stairs as we rededicated the building to God, 100 years after it had first been dedicated as a place of worship.

One guest we were most surprised to see was Ken Tuthill, the shop owner who had turned down our request to use his premises for a charity shop. We had barely paused for breath having opened New Hope House, when already God was revealing something new for the Trust's future. Ken contacted us and said he had changed his mind. God had changed his heart and we could open a shop after all.

Jamie's story

You intended to harm me, but God intended it for good.
Genesis 50:20

Most people don't believe me when I say that becoming homeless was actually the best thing that could have happened to me. I know it sounds bizarre, but my life seemed like a 'hell on earth' up until that point. Losing my house and family acted as the catalyst that turned my life around into the joy that it is now, so I'm glad it happened.

I was the fourth boy born in succession to my parents, who had been desperate to have a sister for their eldest daughter. When I was not the hoped-for girl, my father's disappointment and lack of interest in me was clear. We were living in India as he was in the Indian army, and we came back to England when I was about four. No sooner had we landed than my parents separated, and quickly divorced. My father remarried almost immediately and he and his new wife had a baby of their own – this time the girl my father had wanted for so many years. I felt like a dead tree stump in the garden, superfluous to their new marriage and new family life. There was a big age gap between me and my older siblings from the first marriage, and anyway they had all flown the nest, leaving me with just one true friend in my family circle – Shep, who was a curly-haired black mongrel who hated my father's strict discipline as much as I did.

I didn't see much of my father, who worked long hours in the City. When he returned home from work, he would be shut away from me to spend the evening with my stepmother in the dining room while she fed him and made a big fuss of him. I came quite low down on their list of priorities in terms of attention and even lower in terms of love, kindness and affection. I was desperately lonely and unhappy. I often felt as if I was an alien who had been born into the wrong family, so I'd frequently sneak out of the house and snug up with Shep in his kennel in the garden.

We were nominally a Christian and churchgoing family, and for a couple of years during my mid-teens I was full of religious zeal and got very passionately involved. I'd attend church five times on a Sunday, ringing the bells that called people to worship and singing in the choir. For the first time in my life I felt happy and as though I belonged somewhere. I was suddenly coming top of my class at school and enjoying my studies so much that I was made head boy. Everything was going well for the first time in my life.

But my heart began to grow cold towards Christianity because of the lack of unity in the church. We lived in a wealthy village in Buckinghamshire and the local church congregation seemed more interested in people's class and status than in having a relationship with God. Turning up for church wearing their best Sunday clothes was their definition of being a Christian, and it didn't seem to have any bearing on their behaviour the rest of the week. The surrounding churches fought with each other and among themselves constantly, and I couldn't stand it. Their hypocrisy began to turn me against Christianity. I didn't lose my belief in God – I could still see His glory through the beauty of the world, but I stopped going to church and certainly didn't sit down and pray any more.

I went to college and met a girl called Chris, with whom I quickly fell in love. It sounds a bit naive, but we speeded up the process of getting married as it meant we would get a bigger married college education grant between us than two separate grants, but when she fell pregnant sooner than expected all our financial calculations went out of the window. I was 21 and she was 20, so it was quite a strain on us to be having a family, and our son was an incredibly lively young boy. I was doing a course in photography, but because I needed to provide for my family I had to go back into accountancy where I had started, to make some decent money. I felt I had really missed out by not being able to work in my chosen career as a photographer and this began to put a strain on our relationship. Although Chris found motherhood hard work, she persuaded me that we should have a second child as she really wanted a girl. Of course this just exacerbated our problems and we decided to go our own ways. So we parted amicably with a child each, but this arrangement only lasted about six months as my son missed his mum and his sister so much that it was affecting him at school.

I spent a number of years as a general manager for different companies and went on to work for myself in the financial services industry. I stayed in close contact with Chris and the kids until they moved to Singapore to be with Chris's new husband.

The crisis point came for me in my mid-forties. I was overweight, lived in constant pain from arthritis and had been told it wouldn't be long until I was in a wheelchair or even dead. I was earning good money and enjoyed spending it, but hated the work I did to earn it: it was full of backstabbing and lying and deceit. I'd had enough and didn't want to live the lie that the lifestyle required. I'd tried changing my career and it hadn't helped, so I felt I needed to do something drastic. I'd been living with my girlfriend, Jo, for ten years and while we were happy, I knew I had to make very big changes in my life. It didn't feel fair to impose them on her as she was achieving her life's dream of setting up her own business and I was talking about heading out on a road of uncertainty. I had to leave peers and old friends behind as I knew they would only pull me back to the lifestyle that was killing me. I felt I had two choices: to cast my dinghy onto uncharted waters or to go down with the ship, so I chose the former and gave up everything. I packed up my business and walked away from my old life. I said goodbye to no one but Jo, and set off with just the bare minimum of cash and no idea what I was going to do.

Although it was a terrifying thought, I decided I had more to gain than to lose as I headed out into the unknown. Previously I had owned a house with Jo. Now I just slept on the floors of people I met. I left my steady income and survived by finding bits of cash-in-hand work here and there, often in restaurants. I changed my diet from the rich food and wine that had taken me to 15 and a half stone and became fascinated by the philosophies behind the Hindu eating habits of the gurus. Although I was still adamantly anti-religion, I moved to a Hindu monastery and became more intrigued by the phenomenal control the Hindu gurus were able to exert over their bodies. Never having had much control over myself – hence my weight problem – it had a great appeal. They were so dedicated. When I saw the yoga they practised, I was stunned – it was nothing like the exercises I'd seen Westerners practise. Without building up huge muscles they were able to contort into the strangest positions and hold them for long periods of time.

After a while I realised this new life wasn't the answer to my problems, but it was too late to go back to what I'd had before. I'd burned all my bridges. The path ahead of me was too hard: I didn't know where I was going or what I was doing, and I lost all sense of direction and purpose. My future looked bleak and I couldn't face it, so I made up my mind that would be it. I didn't want to exist and the only thing to do was to take my own life. I planned it all in my head. I'd go to the States and get a gun, find a cliff face overlooking a luscious forest and put a bullet through my head, leaving my body to fall into the trees below. I wanted to be surrounded by beauty as I died and I didn't want anyone to find my body. I hated the idea of an inquest, of my family being asked to identify my body, of people picking over my life and what had happened. I wanted to disappear, to be gone with no traces. I felt that it was no one's business but mine.

So I booked my flight and headed off to America, naively assuming I could pick up a gun as easily as buying a Big Mac. It took some doing, but eventually I got hold of one after seeing an ad in the equivalent of *Loot* and handing over a bundle of cash to a stranger in a seedy hotel.

In my head I was a condemned man and nothing was going to stop me doing what I wanted to do. I can be very determined at times and was clinical in my approach. I went off in search of the ledge I'd imagined, driving down the east coast of America from New York to the Florida Keys. As days turned into weeks and I was unable to find the spot I needed, I grew unsettled; I was letting myself down by not following through on my plan. If I couldn't find what I was looking for, I'd have to find some other way of doing it and disappearing.

When I discovered a reservoir somewhere in Virginia I thought I'd found a suitable alternative place, with a huge dam, deep water and sprawling woods. As I walked among the trees I saw a 15-foot jetty sticking out over the water and I knew that if I killed myself there I could disappear into the dark, deep water and never be found. All I needed was something to weigh my body down so that it would sink into the deep water. I bought two large rucksacks, strapped one on my front and one on my back, and as I walked towards the jetty through the woods I loaded the rucksacks with heavy rocks. I stood on the edge of the concrete jetty looking at the water, focused on the fact that all the pain would soon be over. I fired two shots into the water to make sure the gun was working and then slowly moved the gun up towards my head. As I breathed what I thought would be my last breath, suddenly both the rucksacks burst open at exactly the same moment. Rocks crashed around my feet and bounced into the water of the reservoir, leaving me standing there with just the straps on my shoulders. I couldn't help but laugh at how ridiculous it was! The laughter made me realise the huge amount of tension in my body, and my failed attempt made me feel I'd been knocked a step down the ladder in achieving what I'd planned.

I felt that the reservoir hadn't been a complete loss, though – it had given me the idea that water would be a good place to disappear. But the strange thing was that, no matter how many ways I tried to end my life, something always went absurdly wrong at the last minute. I hired a 30-foot yacht to sail myself out to sea, making sure it had a self-steering gear so that once I was overboard it would keep on going right out to sea, so that it wouldn't direct people to my body. I had few possessions at this point (I gave most of them away as I had no long-term need of them), but I went through a small ceremony of sorts, throwing my final valuables overboard, including an expensive Kenwood personal stereo that had been keeping me company in the previous weeks. With them gone, I stood on the edge of the yacht and leaned out over the water, hanging on to the rigging, gun in hand, when a huge wave crashed into the boat, knocking me off balance. As I fell back into the cockpit of the boat, my foot caught in the cable that controlled the self-steering gear and pulled it right out of the electronic control box, rendering the gear useless. Now I just couldn't bring myself to pull the trigger, knowing they would be able to find me close to the boat.

I was beginning to think somebody wanted me to live. After a few more failed attempts near water, I was becoming so freaked out that I hadn't managed to do what I wanted to do that I gave up on the idea of water as a place to end my life and disappear.

I found an abandoned church – one of those old-fashioned American whitewashed wood buildings – that had been burned out. The churchyard was overgrown, so I figured I could easily hide my car round the back in the bushes where it could feasibly stay hidden for months. As I drove round, sure that this time I would be successful, I must have driven over an unmarked grave, as the ground gave way beneath the front wheels of the car and I ended up with my back wheels stuck in the air at a 45-degree angle. I couldn't believe it. The car couldn't have been more obvious if I'd put a blaring siren on it. But this was it; I was all out of options. It was a freezing cold December night and I prowled the graveyard gazing at the starry sky, psyching myself up to the task that lay ahead. After all the varied botched attempts at ending my life, you'd think it would have been easy by now to complete the task, but something was stopping me from pulling the trigger.

I couldn't bear the thought of failing yet again. Even my desire to disappear was outweighed by my need to die. So I went back to the car and pulled out all the packets of painkillers I'd been storing up in case my 'plan A' didn't work. I crawled onto the back seat of the car, no longer caring if they found me or not, just wishing for the whole thing to be over. I crammed the tablets into my mouth, washed them down with some stale water and waited for death to overcome my frozen, aching body and to still my chaotic mind.

I awoke a few hours later, completely disorientated and stone cold, but most definitely alive. Everything was moving in slow motion, but one thought rang clear in my mind: I wasn't going to die. 'That's it,' I thought. 'That was my final attempt. After two months of trying it's all come to nothing. I'm just going to have to live life the best I can and make the most of it.' There was no hope in my mind, just a grim determination that, as I'd failed to kill myself, I had no choice but to go on living to the best of my ability.

After flying back to England on Christmas Eve, it wasn't long before I ended up back at the Hindu monastery again, spending a lot of time contemplating life. I began to realise how full of anger I was. My father had been an angry person and of course he'd been my closest male role model as I grew up, so it had never bothered me that I had such a short fuse. Now I knew that I not only had to change the practical things like my diet, but I also had to find a spiritual peace if I wanted to carry on a meaningful life. Whereas anger had served me well as a weapon to get ahead in the business world, I no longer wanted it to have a place in my life.

I started getting up in the very early hours of the morning, trying to re-establish my relationship with God. When I first walked outside in the moonlight it would be the owls that kept me company, and then as the first light of dawn became apparent the squirrels would appear and forage through the trees for food, followed by the birds who sang to me as the sun came up. I would get up feeling anger burning like a blazing knot in my chest, but the calm at that time of day soothes even the weariest of souls, so a few hours later I would feel nothing but peace. I began to realise that harbouring anger against others doesn't so much hurt them as eat away at your own happiness.

I wasn't very happy at the monastery. I felt that very few of the monks were truly God-fearing; most were selfish and on the hunt for power wherever they could get it. But gradually I came to have a relationship with God again. Eventually I became the temple commander, which meant I ran the place on a day-to-day basis. I dealt with a variety of problems, and when a woman called Gabrielle was brought to me in floods of tears because a man at the temple was hassling her, it was down to me to help sort it out. The man concerned believed that Gabrielle had agreed to marry him and she had run away, refusing to talk to him. She said it was all in his mind and we believed her. Either way, it wasn't on that he was hounding her. When I managed to persuade him to leave her alone, I guess I became her knight in shining armour.

It was never my intention to get involved, but she made me feel needed and looked up to me in a way that touched my heart. We began to spend more time together and she told me how badly she'd been treated by men all her life. She wasn't very stable and I had many concerns about her character, but she assured me that if we were together and had children she could grow into the person she'd always wanted to be. While I was in the temple I'd missed my children so much that my desire to have a family, which had been denied me since losing contact with my first two children, came back in full force. I felt bereft without them and missed them so much. Gabrielle and I decided to get married and have a family, which meant I had to leave the monastery.

Sadly, it was only after we had our two children that I realised things were seriously wrong. I felt she used our children manipulatively, and there appeared to be a history of such behaviour in the past. She was volatile and would throw temper tantrums over the smallest of circumstances. She even did so in front of the kids, frightening them so much that one hid under a cushion for two hours after a particularly bad episode.

I felt I couldn't continue to live like this, especially given the effect it was having on the children. I wanted to live nearby so that I could still have a good influence on my children's lives, but hoped that if I took myself out of the house, her temper would calm down. Once I left, Gabrielle panicked, fearing I would have the children taken away, even though I told her time and again that this wasn't what I wanted for them. She set out to disgrace and ruin me. She went to our doctor, a solicitor and the health-care worker and told them I was abusing her and the children. I came home to find the house empty as she'd disappeared with the kids and I had no idea what was going on until an agent of the court knocked on the door. He handed me a huge envelope, the letter inside detailing all her accusations and saying I had to leave the house within a week. I was shocked to the core. I had never laid a finger on my wife and I loved my children more than life. I was devastated that anyone could believe I would do such things. To be accused of something so despicable, something I would never dream of doing, something I despised and something that would make people suspicious of me for evermore – it was beyond the realms of my comprehension.

A week later the case came to court and I agreed with the judge that I would leave our home, as the family had nowhere else to go. I went to the local councils in surrounding areas and they all told me the same story: as a single man I wasn't their problem. Gabrielle had frozen my bank account, so I had no money and no means with which to get a place to stay. With just 48 hours to go until I was made homeless, I went to the council again. Desperate, I told them I wasn't leaving their offices until they helped me find somewhere to stay. The housing officer was dismissive.

'It's nothing to do with us,' she said calmly. As the afternoon wore on, she started to get cross as I refused to move. Just before 5 o'clock she got up from her desk, turned on her heels and marched out of the room without a word.

'She's going to call the police and I'm going to be in even bigger trouble,' I thought. I considered leaving, but decided to stay and see it through, as I had nowhere to go anyway.

Fifteen minutes later she came back in and handed me a scrap of paper. 'You can see these people tomorrow and they might be able to help you,' she said. It was my last night at home, so I desperately hoped that they could, or I didn't know what I would do.

I left my home at 8am the following morning, as I had agreed at court, clutching the piece of paper with the address of New Hope House on it. My appointment wasn't until 10am, so I had two hours to kill, wondering whether they'd be able to help me and, if not, where I would go and what I would do. The interview was quite in depth and I found it very emotional telling them what had led to me being homeless. At the end of the interview I was asked to leave and give them some time to consider my case. I went off, racked with nerves, frantically pacing the nearby roads, but when I returned they greeted me with a smile. They told me there was indeed a bed for me and if I wanted to stay and have lunch with them right then, I was very welcome. The relief overwhelmed me – the first ray of light in the midst of such a turbulent week.

I hadn't heard of New Hope Trust before, but I soon came to understand that they were a group of Christians. They had asked me about my beliefs during the interview and, while I still considered myself to be a Hindu, they realised that I had a relationship with and respect for God. I moved into the house and saw there were always news sheets around from local churches and leaflets about the work they were doing to help people in Watford. In addition, volunteers from local churches regularly came and helped out. It was such an eye-opener for me. All those years ago I'd walked away from the church because of the hypocritical attitudes of the people I'd met there – and suddenly I was surrounded by Christians who were living out the gospel by trying to do positive things to help one another.

While I was settling in at New Hope House, my wife was seeing various agencies and making more wild accusations. It was the most terrifying time of my life. In these cases you have to prove that you're innocent rather than someone else prove that you're guilty. It's understandable and right that the law must do all it can to protect children and vulnerable partners, but in a situation like mine where the accusations had no grounding, no medical evidence or history of abuse, it was both unbelievable and unbearable being on the end of such suspicion. Day and night, fears stampeded through my head.

Would I ever be able to work again? Would I end up in prison? Would I always have to see that look in people's eyes, suggesting that they didn't trust me and believed the lies to be true? Worst of all, would I ever be allowed to see my kids again? I thought I was ruined and had no idea how I was going to prove I had never touched my wife or children. Other people at the temple would sympathise with me and even mention other concerns they'd had about Gabrielle. But none were willing to write to the court on my behalf, as they felt the Hindu religion meant that they left the judging to a higher power and shouldn't take sides. I felt so completely and utterly alone, and terrified at what the outcome and consequences might be.

At New Hope House a guy called Albert would come to play pool and chat with residents. He was a local doctor and I enjoyed his company and intelligent conversation. One night in early November he told me he was off to a friend's house to eat Peking duck. I'd been a vegetarian for many years at that point and hadn't wanted to touch meat the whole time, but as soon as he said 'Peking duck' my taste buds went into overdrive. My mind was flooded with one thing: the idea of good food and good company.

'What's the chance of me coming with you?' I asked, licking my lips, fully aware I had no money to pay for such luxuries.

'Someone's pulled out, so I'm sure it would be OK if you came,' said Albert.

He didn't have to say it twice. I was out of the door so fast that he barely had time to blink!

We drove out to Chipperfield, a leafy village a few miles from Watford, and pulled up at a beautiful converted barn. I was introduced to our hosts, Jez and Lynzy, who were new to the area and were going to lead this 'cell group' for the Soul Survivor Church in Watford. I didn't know what a cell group was, but they explained they were part of a local church and met each week to hang out together, learn from the Bible, chat and pray for each other. Jez and Lynzy had a beautiful family home and they'd laid out a huge table and decorated it with candles and loaded it up with the most delicious Chinese food. I was nervous when I realised it was a church meeting, but everyone was so friendly that I soon felt completely at home and I got lost in the enjoyment of such a convivial evening, which I so desperately needed. The duck was fabulous. But what impacted me most was that the people were so beautiful and kind and friendly that I wanted to come back the following week, even if they didn't have duck again! So I went back the following week, and then the next, and as I got to know people I began to wonder whether they were the exception in the church, or if the congregation was made up of the same kind of genuine people.

I still had quite an adventurous spirit, so the idea of checking out the church seemed quite natural to me, despite my reservations as to what Christians could be like. The congregation at Soul Survivor met in a converted warehouse, so there wasn't much to distinguish it as a church except for the huge, rugged wooden cross hanging in front of the stage. I'd gone in expecting pews, hymn books and a quiet and contemplative atmosphere. Instead there were chairs, lively songs led by a band and a very un-vicarishlooking guy up front leading the service.

I was amazed to find that people were warm and friendly and seemed to really back up their words of worship to God in their actions. I was desperately in need of friends, people who wouldn't judge me on the basis of the accusations my ex-wife was making, so it was wonderful to be welcomed in and accepted by the church family. My relationship with Jesus took a while to develop and it started with me realising what a pig's ear I had made of my life. My heart was so hardened against Christianity, and I was so obstinate, that I thought I knew what was what and nothing was going to change my mind. But I believe God used my previous religious experiences as a halfway point where in His grace He spoke to me and led me to the place where I was ready to accept Him and give my life fully to Him.

I'd always known the value of being good, even from a young age. I would get frustrated with myself whenever I did anything wrong, but I felt powerless to fight it or to do anything about it. The difference in going to church again was that I heard about Jesus properly for the first time and I realised that He was what made the difference. I began to see and know Jesus as my Saviour who sacrificed everything, my mentor, guide, example, shining light; He was the essential difference that turned my life around. Having been involved with various religions, I know that although each one felt right at the time, it also felt as if something was missing. I now know that something was of course Jesus Christ and the Holy Spirit.

While I was growing in my faith, life wasn't without other new challenges. Not long after I joined New Hope House I had some problems with my teeth, the upshot being that I had three anaesthetics in as many weeks while they pulled one tooth out, filled another and drained an abscess. I was in terrible pain, one side of my face was completely swollen and it all took its toll on my body. My sleep pattern had been all over the place since I arrived at the house. Unable to cope with the stress of my ex-wife's accusations, I'd stopped living by the normal night and day routine. I sometimes sat up all night and then passed out with exhaustion during the day. It was all too much. For more than a month every movement was sheer agony, even breathing was almost unbearable. I could hardly walk for months and it was a long time until I was fully back to normal.

Just before Christmas, during an early morning Bible study session at New Hope House, we were looking at the account of Jesus being arrested and His trial. Clive, who was taking the session, asked us, 'Can you imagine what it feels like to be wrongly accused? To have the finger pointed at you when you've done nothing wrong and to be thrown into prison on the mere strength of false accusations?'

I didn't have to imagine. My mind shifted to the week before when I'd had a visit from the police to interview me about accusations of theft that Gabrielle had made. I was taken to the police station and thrown in a cell. Finally they got me in an interview room with a number of officers, pushed a tape recorder across the desk to capture our conversation and proceeded to grill me. Thankfully it soon became clear that the accusations were a load of rubbish and I was allowed to go – but not without me knowing again first hand what it feels like to be accused of something you didn't do. What our Bible reading that morning had reminded me of once again was that any suffering we can go through, Jesus can identify with, as He has suffered it and worse.

The work ethic was still burning strongly inside me, so doing nothing because of my illness was driving me crazy. I heard that New Hope Trust was looking for clients who would be interested in helping out with the annual report. I was the only one who came forward, so they took me on to their committee and I started working directly with the charity's chairman and director and other members of the funding and PR department. It was such a blessing to do something that didn't require the physical effort my body wasn't strong enough to handle, but nevertheless gave me an opportunity to use my brain and show I was capable. I was still in great physical pain and many of the meetings were very hard for me to attend, but I persevered because I saw it as a way to begin to repay New Hope Trust for all they were doing for me. Eventually, when the annual report was completed, I was asked to write a personal letter to accompany the report when it was mailed out to all our supporters and potential supporters. My self-esteem had plummeted over the previous year, so it was amazing to be involved with something worthwhile. I felt so lucky to be involved and so pleased to be repaying a debt of gratitude.

After 14 months of living at New Hope House, a studio flat became available through the council. The court was about to grant me access to the children and I knew I needed somewhere to stay, so although the flat was tiny I knew I couldn't wait to see if something better came up. At the same time one of the trustees asked me if I'd be interested in working for the Trust. I couldn't believe that they wanted me! One of the charities that had received the letter I'd written with the annual report was so moved by what I'd written that they wanted to fund a new position at the Trust and, by a miracle, that money was then used to employ me. For the next two years I worked as an assistant supervisor in the woodwork and furniture recycling shop. The position was only four days a week and I needed a full-time job to support myself, so I also worked one day a week in the night shelter. It felt great to be able to help others who were in the same position that I'd been in, and I encouraged as many of the guys as I could to come and get involved in the woodwork project.

Last year a job opened up in the fundraising department and, astonishingly, I was given the position as a short-term placement. As my confidence grew, it began to dawn on me that perhaps I could do the job permanently on a full-time basis. I applied for the full-time position and by God's grace I was successful. I'm currently the community funding officer for New Hope Trust, helping to raise money by organising events that will bring in the funds which are so vital for the continuation of our work with homeless and disadvantaged people in the area. My job is to work with churches, schools, local groups, Scouts, the Boys' and Girls' Brigade, and anyone else who's interested in setting up fundraising events to raise awareness of and money for New Hope Trust.

With God's help I've been able to forgive Gabrielle and to realise that she also is a person in need of help. I was cleared of all the charges she brought against me and I can't help but think of the story of Joseph. Having been reconciled with his brothers after they sold him into slavery, Joseph tells them, 'You intended to harm me, but God intended it for good' (Genesis 50:20). Given the choice, of course, I wouldn't have wanted to go through those awful months of living under her horrific accusations and having to be separated from my children, but I'm so thankful that through those events I now have a more solid relationship with God.

If New Hope Trust hadn't been there for me, I would have been forced to live on the streets when I so suddenly and unjustly lost my home and family. I've seen how easy it is to get into that downward spiral and what a huge struggle it is for people to make their way back, and I can't tell you how thankful I am that God provided for me and steered me in the direction of the Trust. Everything I have now has been brought about because of being made homeless and the fact that I met God through the care and Christian compassion of the staff and volunteers at New Hope Trust. They saved my life in more ways than one.

I feel as if I owe them my life, and my work is not just a job, but a joyful mission for me as I endeavour to bring the same support to other broken lives, as I was supported and nurtured in my own darkest moments by New Hope Trust.

Alpha Court
opened 2005

Day centre opened 1996

Eddie – one of our
many angels

Jamie abseiling for
charity

Keith woodcarving at the furniture recycling project

Mount Zion for sale, 1992

Outside New Hope House, formerly Mount Zion Chapel

Sister and Peter

Sheila, Tim and Janet

Winner's presentation after the 2006 sleepout

8: Green for go!

Therefore, as God's chosen people, holy and dearly loved, clothe yourselves with compassion, kindness, humility, gentleness and patience ... And over all these virtues put on love.
Colossians 3:12–14

While we were still in the process of renovating New Hope House, we encountered a few difficulties at the coaches. During the winter months the coaches were freezing. Despite the gas fires that were installed, we just could not keep the chill out of the air. The pipes were prone to freezing and bursting and the coaches were starting to show their age after many years of consistent use, looking old and worn. We started thinking about building a new day centre that could provide us with more permanent accommodation.

Sheila and I arrived on site one day as normal to find a notice outside saying that the land where the coaches stood was to be auctioned. I immediately phoned Peter Beckett, the owner, to find out what had happened. He broke the sad news that his company had gone into liquidation and the bank now owned everything. We were devastated for him, after all his kindness to us, that he was having such trouble, and were extremely concerned as to what would happen to the coaches. The bank was auctioning off the land in a month's time and we did not know what to do. We had always had the feeling that God had given us the land not just as a temporary home, but as a place that he could use long term. We had heard about a godly couple who had walked past the site many years before we came along and claimed it for the work of God's kingdom, and we were greatly encouraged. 'It's your land, God,' we said and tried to keep our faith that things would be OK.

The day came for the auction and we got all the churches that had supported us to pray that God would do something. I called Peter at the end of the day with my heart in my mouth, but was about to be given another lesson to remind me that praying can make the impossible happen.

'You'll never believe it,' Peter said. 'The site you're on was the only lot – out of 20 – that didn't reach its reserve price!' We all came together to thank God and sing his praises. He had done it again.

The bank wanted £95,000 for the plot and we were still busy raising money for New Hope House. So we asked SAHA whether they could purchase the land and we could pay them back over time. They offered to put in an application to build four flats at the front that we could use for single homeless people, leaving the back free for us to build on. 'It's a late application,' they warned us, 'so it will be divine intervention if we get permission.' But sure enough, permission was granted. We had to move the coaches so they could build, and two of my neighbours, who happened to be trustees of a local sports club, said we could use their land for the coaches until we had built the new day centre and could get rid of them. It was just around the corner from where we were, so it could not have been more perfect. Thank You, Lord, You are amazing!

Just before we moved the coaches we had a very interesting visitor. We were always looking for ways to promote the Trust and so gain support and raise awareness of the problem of homelessness. I had heard that Jeffrey Archer was coming to Watford to speak at a literary lunch at the Hilton Hotel, so I wrote to him and said he would be seeing some of the best of the town at his lunch; would he like to come and see the other side of it? We were delighted when he came back to us to saying yes, and he joined us at the coaches to meet the guys and girls and see what was going on. He really engaged with the men and women and was very friendly – even when one of them gave him some verbal abuse! We did not take any photos or invite the local press, as we did not want it to come across as a patronising publicity stunt for Jeffrey, but we told the newspapers afterwards and they ran the story, which raised awareness for us. Jeffrey has continued to support us over the years, responding to requests for gifts for us to auction during fundraising initiatives. It is a side of Jeffrey Archer that few get to hear about.

Media interest also gave us a great opportunity to speak about Jesus, and during this time one of our early supporters told us she had a contact at *Take a Break* magazine who would like to speak to us. From doing this interview we were invited to speak on Radio 4's *Woman's Hour*. We made it clear that we were Christians and that our faith was a vital part of what we were doing and they seemed happy with that. They came down and interviewed Sheila and me, plus a few of the lads. It was a fantastic opportunity to give God glory for all that He had been doing and to encourage others that they could make a difference in their own towns and cities.

Once the coaches had been moved and the land was ours, we had to get a new day centre up and running. After the lads had been so good at getting involved with our previous endeavours, we thought a self-build project would be a good idea. We knew we did not want the building to look like a social services office; it had to be welcoming and make everyone who came feel at home. A friend suggested we look at London City Farm, so Sheila, Tim and I went there and loved how environmentally friendly their building was.

At around the same time I went to the SAHA AGM and 'just happened' to meet a man called Terry Joy. As we spoke and I told him about our vision he said, 'I'm an architect and my speciality is environmentally friendly buildings. Can I help you plan your building?' He introduced us to Steven Backes, who worked with teams from VSO (Voluntary Service Overseas) and volunteered to become our project manager. We were delighted. Steven was much more qualified than we were to lead the project and we knew he would do a great job. Terry helped us plan a grass roof that would be fed by recycled water from a pond and suggested we have the walls insulated with shredded newspaper.

It took about ten months to complete the building work and Steven managed to use not only the local lads who were keen to help, but also international teams. We were thrilled as groups came from all over the world to help us build the day centre. They came from Europe, Belarus and America. They slept on the floor at St Mary's Church and faithfully laboured each day, staying for anything from one week to one month.

We also had extra hands in the form of our four new assistant project workers (APWs). We had a vision to get young people involved with the Trust, working at all the different projects and learning all they could about caring for the homeless. We rented them a house, paid their bills and gave them pocket money in return for their work. The idea was that they spent a gap year with us, but many loved their work so much that they stayed on and became members of the permanent staff after their year was up. Rob Edmonds was one of the first APWs we had on board and he has been with us for ten years now! We had a great team and they were willing to get involved with anything and everything – and one of their first jobs when they arrived was to pick up paintbrushes and get the day centre ready for business.

The day centre building itself was newsworthy because of its environmentally friendly approach. It drew a lot of attention, even winning the Civic Prize for sustainability. We wanted to provide the same facilities as at the coaches, but now had the option to do so much more. We put in showers and laundry facilities and arranged for a regular drop-in from a GP to give medical advice, as well as visits from dentists, opticians, chiropodists and hairdressers; we started art workshops, crèche facilities and toddler groups to help the young mums, and provided a computer room and a clothes store.

Chris Evans has been one of our volunteers since we first began the coaches. She has stayed with us ever since and after 12 years became a project worker at the day centre. As someone who has been there through so much, I asked her about her experiences. The rest of this chapter contains her recollections.

We have met many amazing men and women through the day centre over the years. Some have come in for just a couple of days during a moment of hardship and then moved on; others have visited us regularly for many years and see us as their first port of call in a crisis. Often people have turned up bleeding and bruised – instead of going to A&E, they have come straight to us; or if they have an emotional crisis, their first thought is to come to the day centre. It takes six paid staff and around a dozen volunteers each week to look after the 70 or so men and women who come in each day.

Although there are fewer female rough sleepers overall, we have seen an increase in the number of women using our services in recent years and also many younger ones. In fact, we have realised that there has become no such thing as a stereotypical day centre client any more. Some are well presented, others stand in rags, some have never held down a job in their lives, others are still currently employed and desperately need help to hang on to that job while they work out their living arrangements.

There have been many amazing things over the years. For me one of the greatest joys is being able to share my faith so freely. I became a Christian just a few years before I came to New Hope Trust and knew that I wanted to express my faith in deeds as well as words. I love that every day we read from the Bible and pray before we eat – just setting the tone that what we are doing is all part of the love of God. There is a real practical element to our work in giving people food and drink, clean clothes and practical training, but much of our time is spent talking to them and building relationships. We are careful not to discriminate on grounds of religion, but equally feel free to answer questions about our faith when they come up. We do not have to force God into conversations, as God opens amazing doors for us to speak of His love. Often people come to us at their lowest point, so of course they are asking questions and seeking to understand more. I have had grown men, whose reputations are fierce and who terrify many people, cry in front of me about the state of their lives. It is a privilege to be the person they talk to, especially when they ask us for prayer, which they so often do. It makes an impact on people that the workers and volunteers are showing them God's love in a practical way. It changes their perception of God as a judgemental and angry father figure. It is an amazing privilege to help people on their journey of faith, to answer their questions, to pray with them and many times to lead them to faith and see their relationship with Jesus grow.

There is a really strong community feel at the day centre, with strength of feeling among the clients akin to that between family members. Sometimes it feels as if we are parents disciplining children as we have to set boundaries for those with chaotic lifestyles. One lad who used to come in a lot – Terry – was 30, but would act like a petulant child. He would stare at me and light up a cigarette to defy the no smoking rule, or try to take extra cakes to have with his tea. Like a parent, you cannot afford to be a pushover! If he overstepped the mark, we might need to ban him for a few days and he would always come back wanting to check that we still loved him and wanted him around. He was a lovely guy, but it was painful to see how insecure he was. He told me his mother had never stopped him doing anything he wanted and he appreciated that we were firm with him, establishing safe boundaries for him.

One of the hard things of becoming like family is that you share in everyone else's pain. Sometimes one of the guys will be doing really well and seems to be getting back on his feet, then he will receive bad news and will go downhill rapidly. It is so hard to watch, knowing there is only so much we can do to help. Sadly, we also have to grieve the loss of some of our 'family members'. Recently there have been two deaths among our regulars and it shook us all up very badly; that is one of the hardest parts of our work.

Stella was just in her early twenties when she died. She had been coming to the day centre most days for about five or six years, so we knew her well. She started her life in Brazil, but came to England at a young age when she was adopted and in her late teens moved to Watford to be with her partner. She was a beautiful girl, both inside and out, but she had terrible problems. Stella had a daughter who was put into foster care and she was only able to see her once a week because of her chaotic lifestyle. In many ways she was still a child herself, unsure of how to take care of her own needs, let alone anyone else's. Social services set her tasks to try to get her to learn about looking after a child, such as bringing lunch for her daughter. Invariably she would just turn up at the day centre minutes before her scheduled appointment and ask us to provide a sandwich and juice, as she had no money left herself. We helped her in every way we could: we started giving her the food and drink and then began to challenge her to work out her budget and keep enough money back to be able to get something herself. It is great to provide a service, but the idea is not that people just become dependent on us: we want them to grow and learn how to handle responsibility.

Stella also had a social worker and for a while she seemed happier. After a spell in the night shelter she got rented accommodation, but she would always invite other homeless people to come back. When the landlord threatened to evict her if she continued, she told them they could not come over any more and in protest those whom she had tried to help burned the house to the ground. Stella lost everything except the clothes she was wearing and was lucky to escape the burning flames herself.

Stella was fascinated with God and how he could heal people, particularly those who had suffered from addictions in the way she had. She gave her life to God and would eagerly chat about Him to volunteers and staff at the centre. But her life was very up and down and gradually the drugs took hold again. She longed to help others and her greatest desire was to be a missionary. Just a few days before she died she was sitting at the day centre, her usual spark apparent, dressed beautifully as always. We could not have been more shocked or upset to hear that she had died from an accidental overdose; such a tragic waste of a young girl's life.

In the same week we lost another regular from the day centre, Al. He was in his late fifties, but when you looked at Al you would estimate that he was nearer 70. We had known him for more than 15 years when he died, and much of that time he had spent sitting in a chair either making cheeky remarks or grumbling at those around him. He would challenge rules and boundaries, which led to heated arguments, but he would always come back to us later to put things right. He was a long-term alcoholic and it took us a long time to piece together a few details of his life. Previously he had been a dustman, and at one point he had had a family, although he lost a child at a tragically young age. He told very few people about that. You cannot help but feel privileged to work with people like Al when you know they trust you with their closest secrets; in fact, for many, you may be the only one who listens.

Somehow Al ended up on the streets, but he seemed to enjoy sharing a tent with friends. We worried about him as winter approached; it was cold and he was not a young man. I kept telling him he needed a home, but he would always reply with a smile, 'This is the life for me.' He did eventually accept a place at the night shelter and from there went into privately rented accommodation. For many of the guys this is the turning point, but it is hard when their friends are also struggling with the same issues. Like Stella, Al invited his street friends into his flat and it got him evicted. For Al, his friends on the street were like family – having his own place meant he was separated from them and he hated that. We have realised over the years that many people who have been homeless find it hard in proper accommodation, as they get lonely. The more time they have on their own, the more they tend to think about what they have lost in the course of their lives, and the pain can be overwhelming.

It was Al's cider drinking that landed him in hospital. There was a great sadness when we received the call saying he had gone in, as we knew his body was not strong enough to pull through. Joy, our day centre manager, went to visit him in hospital, and it was quite an emotional encounter. For the first 10 or 15 minutes she was there, he lay seemingly unconscious. When Joy told him she was going to speak with a nurse, he opened his eyes wide and, although he could not talk at this stage, he pressed his hands together to ask her to pray for him. Joy could see in his eyes that he knew the end was coming, but in asking her to pray he was turning to God in a way he had not done during the rest of his life, and he seemed to be bathed in the peace of God. It was so sad to hear of his death – we had lost another family member – but we were thankful we could be there for Al during 15 tough years of his life and show him God's love.

Strange as it may sound, I think some of our greatest 'success stories' at the day centre may well be the ones we know very little about. I like to think about the people who come through whom we only see once or twice. They have suddenly found themselves without accommodation, and if they want to hold down their jobs and get themselves back into a home, they need to stay presentable. Obviously that is very hard for people on the streets, but we can provide a place for them to have a shower and wash their clothes so they can keep their job. It is a very small and simple thing, but it can make all the difference between someone finding themselves in a downward spiral and being able to sort the crisis out quite quickly.

There are also many stories like Sally, who when we first met her was heavily into drugs and alcohol. She was always spaced out and would sit with her equally drugged-up boyfriend, barely able to talk to anyone. There was an incident when she almost took her own life, but I think the scare was actually what she needed as it motivated her to go back to rehab. She split up with her boyfriend, which was a big help in keeping her away from a lifestyle of drink and drugs. When she had finished her detox, she came back to Watford and did factory work. We worried that seeing people she knew and used to take drugs with would be hard for her, but she was really strong and has stayed clean. She is now in a much healthier relationship with a really nice guy and has completed the 'Back to Work' course we run here at the day centre. It was such a brilliant feeling to see Sally doing so well, wanting to get on with her life and being able to put her CV together and apply for jobs.

It is a real privilege seeing people rebuild their lives through working at the day centre. It is not always easy, but God has called us to what we are doing and He gives us the compassion and grace we need to love everyone who comes through the door as best we can.

9: Second-hand experience

God can do anything, you know – far more than you could ever
imagine or guess or request in your wildest dreams!
Ephesians 3:20 (The Message)

Having our first charity shop proved to be a blessing in more
ways than one. We knew that selling quality second-hand
goods could provide us with vital income, but it also gave us a
fantastic opportunity to reach out to members of the
community we otherwise would not have met. When we were
first given the keys to the shop, I took my sister Ann, who has
spent her whole life working in retail, and we stood in the shop
praising God for the way he had turned the landlord's heart
around. There and then I asked Ann if she would run the place
for us, and thankfully she agreed. We looked around the bare
shell and began to list in prayer all the things we needed to
transform the room into a shop: clothes rails, dressing rooms,
cabinets, tills and shelves, not to mention goods to sell.

I phoned Watford property services on the off-chance that
they had any shop fittings going spare. They told me that a
jeans shop had recently gone out of business, so they suggested
we meet there and see if there was anything left that we could
use. As I entered the shop I could not believe it: all the fixtures
and fittings Ann and I had prayed for were there! 'Let's have a
quick look upstairs and see if there's anything else,' the
property services manager suggested, but I already knew we
had everything we needed. To my amazement, however, God
had another surprise waiting for me. Upstairs there were
hundreds of pairs of brand-new branded jeans that we could
use as stock. I could not believe it and praised God that He so
often not only provides for our needs, but also gives us more
than we can even ask for. It was a great way to open the shop

with such good-quality merchandise, and when the local churches heard what we were doing, people volunteered to help and to donate goods, so we had a good amount of stock.

The funds provided by the shop are used for the day centre and, having moved to much larger premises in recent years, the shop continues to bring in more than £150,000 a year and has a team of 26 volunteers. There is a chapel area where staff pray every morning and ask God to send people in who are in need of a chat or would like to be prayed for, and these encounters are common. Some of the homeless men and women come in for a cup of tea and to collect their 'starter packs'. The shop makes these up every time someone we know moves into a new home and has no material goods. Gathered from donations to the shop, the packs contain all the necessities such as bedding, towels, pots and pans, cutlery and mugs.

Polly, who currently manages the shop and has volunteered there for the last ten years, goes by the motto, 'Give the best and God will make up the rest', so she often gives goods away at cheaper prices when she knows that someone cannot afford them. Perhaps unsurprisingly, she tells how, often, minutes later someone will offer to overpay for an item, making up the exact cost she just lost.

All manner of weird and wonderful items are given, and the strangest thing is that they get sold! False teeth were donated, which turned out to be perfect for a customer studying dentistry; a single bicycle wheel came in one day, followed by a creative person the next day who wanted to use it for a mobile in their garden. The workers all laughed when a fox's skull was donated, but sure enough it was perfect for a child's school project and a very happy mum took it home with her. One of our favourite stories from the shop is about their 'underpants miracle'. One day they received a call from the workers at the shelter saying they needed about 40 pairs of men's underpants – did they have any? They checked their stock and said no, but promised to pray and ask God to provide. Later that same day they sorted through a few sacks of donated clothes and, sure enough, in the last bag they found exactly 40 pairs of men's underpants!

One day Pat, who runs a shop just down the road from ours, came in looking flustered. She grabbed me by the hand and said, 'Janet, we have to do something!'

'About what?' I asked.

'I've just seen Chris [one of our regulars at the coaches]. He was passed out in a doorway and a young lad was urinating on him. It's disgusting; we've got to help him!'

I felt sick to my stomach that anyone could do something so despicable and felt that familiar sensation that we needed to provide more than we were currently. While we wanted to help people to get over their addictions as much as possible, we were fully aware that some of them had no desire to stop drinking or taking drugs. They just were not at a stage where that was feasible, but hearing about Chris made me realise again that we needed to provide them with somewhere safe to stay.

I noticed that a property backing on to my house was empty and called the council to see if we could use it for a very small amount of rent. They agreed immediately – and we had a community home for our long-term rough sleepers! Noleen, one of our staff members whom the lads adored for her easy-going Irish nature, came and ran the house, which had room for five people at a time. It was a 'wet house', so the men did not have to give up alcohol completely, although their intake was monitored by Noleen and her team and the idea was to try and help them reduce their drinking over time. Over the first year 43 people stayed – some for a few nights; others for months at a time. For many, staying at the house gave them the strength to go on to formal detox and rehabilitation places, but the sad truth is that there were also those who could not cope and so chose to leave to be able to continue drinking 24-7.

One amazing man we had stay with us was Pete Hunt. He had suffered many losses in his life and consequently became homeless and a chronic alcoholic. Pete always stuck in the memory of anyone who met him, as he was a genuinely larger-than-life character. At more than six feet tall and with a broad frame, he looked quite menacing, but he was just a big softy underneath, a real gentle giant. Pete always brought a smile to people's faces with his amazing ability to see the bright side. He came to the house one night with a black eye, but in fits of laughter. When staff asked him what had happened, he explained that his friend Ray had headbutted him. What Pete found hilarious was that Ray had to stand on a wall to do it, as he was only about five feet tall, and so Pete willingly stood there and let him take a shot!

A local church ran a six-month discipleship course for young people and would regularly send people from the course to our projects to work with us during their time in Watford. When Pete came to the community home, we had Naomi, Emilie and Emily who regularly visited at the house from the course. All the guys loved these confident, bright young women and would be on their best behaviour when they were around. A lot of our male workers have said over the years that when there was trouble, the women were often much better at handling it, as the guys would behave themselves, whereas if another man stepped in they would get more aggressive.

When Pete first met Naomi, Emilie and Emily he took an instant shine to them and nicknamed them the 'Spice Girls'. As well as having fun and enjoying teasing everyone, Pete liked to sit and talk about the meaning of life. There were many evenings when Pete would be in tears recounting some of the sadness of his past, or telling of his frustration with his alcohol dependency and his desire to be different and free. This was a great opportunity for the staff and volunteers to share with him their Christian beliefs. It was not long before Pete was going to church, and he grew to love God. You would always know when Pete was there, as he would often stumble in, head for the front row and worship God in song with all he had. His favourite hymn was 'Amazing Grace'. Every time he sang the line 'that saved a wretch like me', he would put his great big fist in the air and punch it to emphasise the truth that the words spoke deep into his heart. He knew in a way that many of us miss in our comfortable lives that he had no hope outside Jesus, and he knew he was saved.

As Pete's relationship with God deepened, he could not help but tell people around him about God and His love. It was a rare Sunday when Pete had not dragged another of the guys along to church with him; he was desperate for those he loved to know God in the way that he did. In the pockets of his thick winter coat he kept his only real possessions – a Bible in one side and a bottle of cider in the other.

He was very thoughtful and once hunted for hours to find a mug that had one of the workers' names on it, Rob, to show him that he appreciated him. Another time he arrived with a necklace as a present for Naomi. It was not a conventional-looking necklace, though – more of an old toilet chain he had found that day! But, in whatever form it took, Pete always enjoyed giving presents and letting people know that he loved them. Despite often drinking up to 18 litres of cider a day, Pete enjoyed helping out around the house, working in the garden and helping to cook meals for the people who stayed there. He would also often be found playing practical jokes on the other guys there and on the staff, so there was never a dull day.

Pete was close to his brother and sister and also a very loyal friend. When one of his close friends, Tim, died, Pete turned up at the funeral with his nails painted black as a sign of mourning. On the way out of the crematorium Pete was scratching his head because he had nits. Emily noticed and offered to get him some ointment to get rid of them, but Pete politely declined. He said it was the last thing Tim had given him and out of respect he thought he should keep them! That night Pete and a few of the other guys slept at the crematorium to keep Tim company and as a sign of solidarity. Pete knew in the truest sense what it meant to be part of a committed community. He may have expressed it in a rather unorthodox way, but nevertheless he was a truly loyal and committed friend.

Things did not always run smoothly for Pete. From the community home he got a flat and for a while was quite self-sufficient. But then there were hard times and he was back with us again. This pattern continued for years, but through it all Pete remained cheerful. He continued to care for those around him, and he always put his trust in God.

Sadly, Pete's addiction took his life in 2003. His funeral was extremely moving. The church was bursting with his family, friends from the streets, staff and volunteers from the Trust and many people from his church. It was obvious to everyone how well loved and respected Pete had been. Naturally the service ended with 'Amazing Grace', although many people could barely get the words out through the lump in their throats when they saw all the homeless guys punch their fists in the air in tribute to Pete.

* * *

With so much happening at the Trust we, as a group of trustees, began to realise that we needed to appoint a chief executive to manage our ever-increasing activities. After a long interviewing process we found the right man for the job: Basil Lazenby. Basil had many years of senior management experience. Prior to joining us he had left the large NHS trust for which he had been working and had spent a year serving his local church and helping them to set up an Alpha course. His experience as well as his heart for God and for people made him the ideal candidate to bring the professionalism we had been seeking.

Basil spent his first few months with us understanding what was going on, how all the projects worked, how they could all work together and where he felt the Trust needed to go. He presented his findings to all the trustees, staff and volunteers and said his view was that we needed a time of consolidation, to firm up everything we were already doing and therefore not to grow for a while. He laughs every time he recalls those words now, as clearly God had other plans! We all felt at the time that although we had been entrusted with the responsibility of the Trust, the reins were firmly in God's hands and we were having to run as fast as we could to keep up with Him.

We had moved our temporary night shelter (the mattresses on the floor) to Oasis House, which provided beds for about eight people during the winter months. What we really needed was to have somewhere that could offer accommodation throughout the year. Although the risks of death through hypothermia are fewer outside winter, there are still many hazards associated with living on the streets for such long periods. Accommodation in Oasis House was a great improvement from the temporary night shelter, with its dining room and lounge, but living space was cramped. The men had to share rooms, often in bunk beds, which did not feel as dignified as we would have liked the accommodation to be.

Around the time that we felt God putting this burden in our hearts to get a new building, we found out that the Salvation Army citadel was going to be up for sale as they had another building elsewhere in the town. It was an ideal location for us, just minutes from the town centre, and the size of the building itself was just right. Funnily enough, we were not the only ones who thought so and the national Salvation Army board took over the sale because of the extensive interest and prime position. We told all our supporters and staff about the building and our plans for it and asked them whether they felt it was the right thing. The overwhelming response was 'yes'.

The SA decided to let people offer sealed bids, and so we prayed hard and felt it was right to offer £185,000, although at that point we did not have a spare penny. I was at the office with Basil when the call came through to say that we were the highest bidder, and the SA wanted us to buy the citadel as we had worked together before and had a similar ethos. We were delighted. But then we heard the news that made our hearts fall to our feet: we had to raise all the money within 28 days in order for the sale to go ahead. We could not believe it but we knew that God had given us this opportunity, and we were not about to lose time worrying when we had some serious fundraising to do.

We contacted all our supporters again, telling them of the latest developments, asking them to pray and to see whether they felt able to contribute towards the costs in any way. Each time we wrote a letter or went to speak to another church group, we used the words of John Wimber that 'faith' is spelt R-I-S-K. We knew it seemed crazy that we might be able to get the money to the SA in such a short time, but we had seen God do amazing things so many times that we knew this was what faith looked like for the Trust.

We sent out a stack of letters on the Friday, and when we met together on the Monday morning to pray, we were stunned to find there was already a response. One of our supporters who worked in the City had just received a large bonus and had been praying about where he could give some money. When he got our letter, he immediately promised us £50,000 which would be gift-aided. Our faith took a great boost that day, and over the following days we watched the money come in as God stirred people's hearts to give to the homeless. One day a young boy knocked on the office door and gave us 50p from his pocket money; that gift was so precious to us. Some days we would take a call offering us an interest-free loan; on other days bundles of envelopes containing cheques would fall through the letter box.

Sure enough, within 28 days we had all the money we needed. When we told the SA we had everything in place, they asked if we had got a mortgage. We were delighted to tell them that we had not even needed to go to the bank: God had provided everything.

Of course, that still left us with a rather large bill, as the church and church hall needed to be converted into living accommodation as quickly as possible. The idea was to make it habitable in the short term and then turn it into more permanent accommodation over the next few years. Basil put us in touch with a group called CRASH, a charitable organisation linked to many of the major building companies. When they got on the case it was like watching a team from a home makeover show in action. We had builders, plumbers, electricians and carpenters all offering their services free of charge, while many of the companies offered us goods such as showers or plasterboard to get the conversion done. In the end we only had to pay for a few items and we had a fantastic night shelter. We thanked God not only for His provision, but also for such wonderful confirmation that this was His plan to make a year-round night shelter. The hall was able to provide 15 beds. They were all separated by plasterboard walls or a curtain, and each resident had their own bedside table and place to store their things.

One of our guests at the night shelter was a young lad called Peter. His parents had asked him to leave home and he had nowhere else to go. It could sound as though they were being cruel, but the truth is that it was the hardest decision they ever made. They were a loving and supportive family, but Peter had become involved with a crowd that encouraged him to take drugs and shoplift. His parents tried to help him, but saw their loving, sensitive son turning into a volatile and aggressive individual who stole from his friends and family and who was sacked from his job. In heartache and desperation they asked him to leave home, knowing that Peter needed something they could not give.

Peter came to us, and during his stay we were able to refer him to the Amber Foundation. They work with young people whose lives are not going anywhere and give them a fresh start, building their self-esteem and encouraging them to gain practical skills and qualifications. One of Peter's dreams was to join the army, and he gained the motivation and self-confidence to apply. He was accepted and has completed his training – and is now doing Royal Guard duty at Buckingham Palace. It was a delight for us to see. Not only did Peter regain his future, but also his parents regained their son. Our part in providing the night shelter is just a stepping stone, but it can keep young people like Peter from ending up on the streets and getting lost in a downward spiral.

We carried on with the temporary night shelter for a couple of years, while working on a more permanent solution with Places for People Housing Association. They drew up detailed plans to redevelop the building and provide eight emergency beds and 'cluster flats'. Cluster flats are a great way of introducing homeless people back into their own accommodation. The flats are set up so that three people can live together – they have their own bedroom and share a kitchen, lounge and bathroom. The flats are supervised by the night shelter staff, so everyone is fully supported in this transitional period. The idea is that they live in this accommodation for a while, getting used to looking after their own space, and eventually becoming ready to move on to their own flat elsewhere.

One of the great things that Basil brought to us as our chief executive was the desire to offer a holistic approach to people's rehabilitation. He wanted to make sure that at whatever stage someone came to us or we met them, whether that be on the streets, through the day centre, night shelter, New Hope House or the community home, they were given every opportunity to move on in their lives, fully supported and encouraged. So much for consolidating – Basil's ideas were about to grow to give us whole new areas of work!

10: The fruits of our labours

Suppose a brother or sister is without clothes and daily food. If one of you says to them, 'Go in peace; keep warm and well fed,' but does nothing about their physical needs, what good is it?
James 2:15–16

Basil's desire to provide a holistic approach to the problem of homelessness got us looking at some new areas of work. His heart was that the Trust should provide a series of stepping stones for anyone at any stage of homelessness. At the time there were people living on the streets of Watford who did not come and access our services. Rather than wait for them to come to us, if they ever did, Basil wanted us to get out to meet them and see how we could help. We now have an outreach team whose job it is to find the rough sleepers in the area, get to know them, offer them support and help them access services either through us or other organisations. Sometimes that means bringing them along to the day centre; at other times it means getting them a place in a rehabilitation centre or perhaps a bed in the night shelter, but the main thing is to engage with them, to build relationships and to show them that someone cares when they are used to being ignored.

At the other end of the scale there were people who had come through the Trust and had moved into their own accommodation, but needed continued support to be able to stay in that place and look after themselves. Basil's idea was for a 'tenancy sustainment team' (TST) to work with those who have moved on, visiting them and keeping relationships going, encouraging them to look after themselves, helping them to access benefits and pay their bills. Moving into a flat can be a lonely time for many people, and the support of the TST can make all the difference in keeping people going and making sure they do not become homeless again.

The team also work with the police and local council to find people who are at risk of being made homeless. If someone can get in before anything happens, there is a greater chance of that individual keeping his or her home and staying off the streets. This may mean representing them in court or helping to organise finances to arrange the repayment of rent arrears. The idea is not to do everything for them, but to help them to do it for themselves. It has been estimated that for every week someone spends living on the streets it will take them a month to get back to normal life, so it is vitally important that we get in at the start and try to stop them becoming homeless in the first place.

It was through some of these new initiatives that Louise Casey (Director of the Homelessness Directorate at the Office of the Deputy Prime Minister) heard about our work and visited us. The work of New Hope Trust was chosen by the government as an example of good practice, and while we were delighted with this acknowledgement, we were quick to tell Louise there was plenty more we wanted to do. She asked if there were any specific projects we had in mind, so we told her about the idea of social businesses where people could get involved in a practical role, learn new skills and build their self-esteem. We were told to put the details down on paper to apply for funding and we won two grants – one for a market gardening project and the other for a furniture recycling and woodwork scheme. The businesses are very simple, but they have proved to be a fantastic aid to the people who get involved.

The community home was blessed with plenty of land at the back and this became the place for a wonderful gardening project. Elaine is our market garden project manager and she works with any of the guys and girls who want to get involved.

It is open to anyone from any element of the Trust (e.g. visitors to the day centre, and those staying at the community home, night shelter or New Hope House), and they also receive referrals from other agencies. Many come because it gives them a distraction from their addictions and problems, an escape from the boredom of the streets or a lonely bedsit. They get involved with everything including digging, weeding, sowing seeds, pruning, harvesting and even selling the assortment of fruit and vegetables that they grow. Some enjoy having the space to think while they work, others the satisfaction of achieving something positive and seeing things grow, and often it is having company and doing something as part of a team that helps.

One guy, Paul, was asked to leave New Hope House as he had been breaking the rules. He was told that if he wanted his place back he should go and stay at the night shelter and work at the gardening project during the day to prove himself. When he arrived he moaned that he hated it, but he persevered and we saw a dramatic change. He began to work really hard and take real pride in what he was doing, painstakingly pulling out weeds that dared to grow around his vegetables. His sense of achievement really helped him during a difficult time. He got his place back at New Hope House and has now gone on to hold down a job and keep his own flat. He proudly told Elaine that he could not wait to grow his own vegetables for his own family in his own garden one day.

Some only come to the gardening project for short periods of time, like those who need the daily distraction of physical work as they wait for places in rehab. Others, like Ian, who lived at the community home for years and worked faithfully in the garden, come back even once they have moved on from a Trust home. The produce is either sold or given to the guys to eat – it is one way of thanking the people who help out on the project, and they benefit from fresh fruit and vegetables in their diet!

We have seen God do many amazing things in the lives of the homeless men and women we have met over the years. But many of our workers and volunteers also have wonderful stories to tell of how they came to be at New Hope Trust and of what God has done in their lives. God began preparing Elaine for the work she is doing at the Trust as the market garden project manager many years before she even gave her life to Him. In fact, you could say that God started giving her a passion for the outdoors at the tender age of two, when she moved with her parents to her grandfather's farm in Bovingdon. Elaine's grandfather would often take troubled young lads under his wing. He let boys who had lost their way and were staying at the local YMCA come and work on the farm, so it was the norm for Elaine to be around people who had difficult issues but were trying to change their lives.

When Elaine reached the age of 16 she started to smoke cannabis, lost her way somewhat and drifted through a number of jobs, gradually losing her self-confidence and motivation in life. She married at 18 and during her twenties gave birth to two boys, Justin and Matthew. While motherhood was a great joy for Elaine, her marriage was rocky and caused her great pain. When her eldest son was 18, Elaine knew she had to leave her husband for good. Matthew was just 11, however, and they did not have anywhere to go, so spent the summer looking after friends' houses while they were on holiday, feeling the pain and insecurity of having no permanent place to live. Eventually they were given a house in Bedmond and Elaine's heart sank – it was not in the nicest area. Looking back now, though, she says she can clearly see that it was God moving her there.

With no certain career path and a need to find a future, Elaine considered her skills and passions, and realised that her greatest love had been tending her garden over the years. During the turbulence of a painful marriage and divorce, Elaine found escape in the therapy of being outdoors, so she started a two-year diploma in horticulture. While the studying went well, her sons splitting their time between their parents was a painful experience for them and something she regretted putting them through. It also left Elaine alone for many weekends and caused great loneliness. She saw an Alpha course advertised, which was being run at a friend's home, and decided she would go along to the weekly lunches for the social aspect, not giving much thought to the spiritual element of the course. One week a young woman came to talk to them and told how she had spent many years living in a camper van travelling around India and smoking pot. As Elaine heard her story there were many parallels with her own, and the tears flowed freely down her face. It was her first experience of the touch of the Holy Spirit. The course helped Elaine on her journey to God and she gave her life to Jesus, joined a local church and became passionate about living for her Saviour.

After college Elaine became self-employed, working on the design and upkeep of local gardens. She also met Dan, whom she later married. In the summer of 2000 Elaine and a friend visited the Hampton Court flower show, where she felt inspired to design a garden that would glorify God. The next day she was working in her garden when a stream of words began repeating themselves in her mind – the name of someone she knew who was a heroin addict, 'therapy' and 'garden'. The words stayed on an endless repeat and an amazing excitement bubbled inside her. That Sunday Elaine spoke to her vicar, Angela, and said she wanted to use gardening as a means of therapy. Angela advised her that the nearest place to do that was Reading, which would have been too far for Elaine to commute. She had no idea how to turn her passion into reality.

After the service Elaine happened to pick up an annual report from a charity she had never heard of before, New Hope Trust, and took it home to read. As she turned the pages she saw a picture of Ian, one of our community home residents, holding a tomato he had grown. Feeling compelled to call, but confused as to why, Elaine picked up the phone and told Nick, the community home worker who answered the phone, about her growing passion. 'I think God's speaking to you,' he said.

Elaine felt confused; she had never experienced hearing from God before and she kept thinking, 'I heard no audible voice; how can God be speaking?' However, she agreed to come to the home and spent the whole journey wishing she could get out of it, wondering what she would say when she arrived. As she was being shown round the garden by Noleen, the home's manager, she was told they had just received funding to employ a project supervisor for the market garden project, working to rehabilitate the homeless guys. Elaine got the job and so has seen how gardening can be used as therapy for many people, including those recovering from addictions.

The furniture recycling scheme has also provided a great opportunity for many of the people with whom we work to gain new skills and rebuild their confidence. Unwanted furniture is donated to us from people all over the place, which we collect. The guys restore it and then sell it on through the furniture shop. They are also trained in many elements of woodwork and carpentry, some even studying at local colleges to gain relevant qualifications. One of the men who has been involved with the project is Keith. This is his story.

More than 20 years ago I lost both of my parents within a month of each other. Unable to cope with living in the house without them, I decided to go to Brighton for a few days' holiday, but I had a nervous breakdown and those few days turned into ten years of living on the streets. I made friends with another homeless man, John, who had left his wife. I did my best to reunite him with his family and get him to go back home. In turn, John encouraged me to come back to Watford, where, having caught a terrible cough and cold, I was admitted to hospital. The doctors asked where I was living, and when I told them my current home was a bus shelter, they put me in touch with New Hope Trust.

I was given a place at New Hope House, where I lived for six months and got back to civilisation. Then they helped me get a bedsit of my own in a nearby village. While living at New Hope House I got interested in the furniture recycling scheme and began working in the woodwork shop. I now have a City and Guilds certificate which qualifies me as a carver, and I'm so proud to be able to say that. I work in the shop four days a week and find it very relaxing. It gives me something to do and I can go away at the end of the day satisfied, knowing I've achieved something.

We have loved seeing the changes in so many people through the gardening project and the furniture recycling scheme. It is often hard to imagine how low your self-esteem becomes after being made homeless, and frequently people start out thinking they will not be able to do the task at hand. Seeing them not only do that task, but also go on to learn greater things, is wonderful, and the resulting increase in their confidence and sense of purpose is amazing. The social businesses have been such a blessing in this way, and our hope is that one day we will be able to hand the projects over to the guys themselves to run as profitable businesses.

Danielle's story

We have this hope as an anchor for the soul, firm and secure.
Hebrews 6:19

I don't remember any good parts of my childhood; in fact, I don't suppose I was a child for very long as my upbringing hardly protected my innocence. My mum was 16 when I was born; my dad had already cleared off and though I know his name, that's all I know about him. My mum couldn't cope with me and went into a deep depression after I arrived. She got involved with the wrong crowd and started taking drugs. My earliest memories are of seeing her beaten up and abused by her so-called friends.

Mum had a stream of people come in and out. I would look around and not recognise a single face in my home and wonder, 'Who are all these people?' It always felt as if I was just 'there', a part of the background but not a part of real life. Even from that age I don't remember feeling much except empty. I watched as Mum's friends talked about 'peace, love and harmony', but all the while they were drinking and taking drugs – they didn't seem to be peaceful to me. The main interaction I had with my mum was when she would scream and shout at me. Then she took to hitting me; I had my first black eye when I was just four years old. She left me with strangers, oblivious to the fact that one boy she left me with sexually abused me when I was seven.

A few years later my mum lashed out at me once too often. She beat me so hard that I ran to my nan, who lived over the road. She took me in and she and Granddad loved me, but they were strict and wouldn't let me go out. Nan worked, so most of the time I had to sit in the house with my granddad. I started

144

missing school, bunking off to go and drink and smoke drugs with my friends. Most people can't believe I was doing that at the age of nine, but it's no surprise when that's the only example you've been shown.

Life didn't get any easier. My nan died from cancer, so not only did I lose her, but it meant I had to move back in with my mum again. All that did was put me in touch with the wrong people, and I took my first sniff of cocaine with Mum's friends at the age of 12.

Mum didn't know. She was having a nervous breakdown, trying to cope with her depression and the loss of her own mother. I didn't even figure on her radar. While she worked in wine bars, I was off getting into trouble. I'd take drugs, then go and start fights with random people on the street. I was so angry and had no way of dealing with it, so I took it out on anyone I could.

When my mum couldn't cope any more, she sent me to a children's home. I thought that the new surroundings might be a good thing, that I might get the security and attention that I craved, but things were no better there. They didn't seem bothered about what I did, so I carried on missing school and taking drugs.

I was fostered by a woman called Nicola. I grew to love her and we had a good relationship, but she was an alcoholic. She was paid to look after me, but she'd take me to the pub with the money she earned and we'd spend the day getting drunk.

Looking back now, I know that I grew up way too quickly. I was trying to act like an adult, to handle the situations that life was throwing at me, but I didn't have the tools to live like an adult at the age of 14. I hung around with people much older than me, and my main concern was to party and to look good. I made sure I was always carefully made up, wore the right clothes, had the right haircut and had money in my back pocket. I thought I looked good and was acting the part, but it was all a front to hide the fact that I was so lost. I didn't trust anyone and I was achingly empty inside.

When I was 16, I left Nicola's and got my own flat in London. I had no qualifications as I'd missed so much of school and I had no prospects. I'd never felt wanted, never known my place in the world, and that didn't look set to change, so I tried to get high every day to forget all of that. I'm ashamed to say that I stole credit cards and lived it up at other people's expense. I had a key worker as I'd left care before I was 18, and she gave me some money to live on, but I spent it on drugs. With my bad attitude I attracted the wrong crowd and spent my time with blokes who thought they were gangsters. We'd go to the best bars and clubs, ordering whatever drinks we wanted, snorting lines of cocaine and thinking we were living like celebrities. When I was all dressed up and had lots of drugs, I'd feel better about myself. I thought that people wanted to hang around me. But when I came down I started to hate myself and feel uncomfortable in my own skin. I kept buying furniture, hoping that being surrounded by nice things would make me feel better about myself, but after a while material possessions just didn't mean anything.

At around this time I made my first visit to a crack house, which is the worst environment you could be in. They're abandoned houses just full of people taking drugs. Once you've been in to see the dealer you're suddenly surrounded by people wanting some of your drugs. I had no idea the whole thing is a trap: the more you get, the more they want. As they pester you it ruins your high, so you go back to get more, and the cycle just keeps going. Stupidly, I took one of the guys who pestered me back to my flat – I was so desperate for company I didn't see what I was getting myself into. He tried to rape me, and in an attempt to defend myself I jumped out of the window, thankfully only breaking a leg. I kept putting myself in these awful situations, but I couldn't find a way out of it.

I met a guy called Mev. I thought I loved him and we started doing crack cocaine in my flat. The drug makes you feel paranoid and so I began to withdraw from society and stopped going out. I didn't care any more and stopped looking after myself. One day I just walked out of my flat and went to live with him. The cocaine wasn't working any more; reality was kicking in too regularly for my liking, suffocating me and reminding me I had nothing. I turned to heroin. It quickly turned into a daily habit that I was desperate to feed. I'd lie, steal, cheat – anything to get the fix that would block everything else out. I'd walk the streets, telling anyone who'd listen that I was desperate. I'd admit the truth, that I was a drug addict, but I'd say that I needed their money to get help and come off the drugs.

I felt totally powerless to control what was happening to me. I was just a slave to my addiction. I left the guy I was living with and had nowhere else to go, so I just went from place to place, trying to find a floor to sleep on at strangers' houses. My daily concern was getting money to feed my growing heroin habit.

Soon I had nowhere to go and spent day and night on the streets. I lost my looks, the drugs were wrecking my body, my skin was pale and taut over sunken cheekbones, my hair was unwashed and hung limply in a straggly mess. Cocaine gives you gum disease, so I'd lost many teeth too. The streets and squats I found weren't safe, and a number of times men tried to rape me. I didn't have the sense to feel scared, though. The drugs numbed everything and so I stayed in this dangerous situation.

I lost all my self-worth. I hadn't bathed in a long time, my clothes were dirty and I know I smelled pretty bad, but I didn't care. I isolated myself, sitting on my own all day just taking my drugs. I was desperate. I hoped there was a way out, but I had no idea how to find it. I didn't know how to face up to the feelings I had inside, so I just kept blocking them out.

When things got really bad I contacted my mum for the first time in months. I had totally lost control and during the first few phone calls I did little more than scream and shout at her, telling her that she never loved me and I hated her for never trying to help me. She was getting her life back together, but that only made me feel more left behind and abandoned as she hadn't included me in this new lifestyle of hers. The truth was, I desperately wanted a relationship with her. I'd spent so long surrounded by strangers, people who took advantage of my naivety and illness, that I knew I needed to be near family. I wasn't romanticising our relationship, but I knew I couldn't be on my own any more and I knew that she was in a better place in her life too. I went round to see her, covered in sweat (one of the withdrawal symptoms of heroin), and begged her for more money. She could see what a mess I was in and she gave me cash, but I wanted something more – I felt palmed off. I took the money and got more drugs, sleeping all day and looking for a fix at night. The only way I knew how to live was to take more drugs, so I'd carry on with the cocaine and heroin, spending days around people who argued violently and hurt each other. I've never felt so empty and alone.

I had lost so much weight as I barely ate anything and was living under staircases with dustsheets wrapped round me to try to keep myself warm. When my mum saw the darkness in my eyes, she realised how serious things had become and saw that I needed help. She got some money together to send me to a rehabilitation place outside London. I knew that if there was a way out of this hellish life, then I wanted to find it.

The centre gave me pills to substitute for my drugs, reducing my dose down and putting me through detox. The withdrawal was excruciating. I felt weak and shaky all the time, had cold sweats all day and vivid nightmares through the night. We had groups to discuss how we got into drugs, but no one ever seemed to address the real issue of what was going on inside.

They were helping to heal me physically, but my emotional and spiritual needs were untouched. At 4 o'clock in the afternoon the groups finished and we were left to go back to normal life. The trouble is, for an addict there's no such thing as a normal life. We all lived in houses nearby (part of the programme), we were in the early stages of recovery and were all weak. When someone suggested going to the pub, we all went along and inevitably got drunk. It may sound strange, but I actually didn't know we weren't allowed to drink. My understanding was that I was at the centre for my addictions to cocaine and heroin. They never told me that as an addict, alcohol could have such a negative impact on my recovery. Using any type of mind-altering substance just sets off the craving again for your drug of choice, but I didn't know that.

We all got kicked out, every single one of us. They just gave up on us and I felt lost and worthless. I started using as soon as I came out – what else was there for me? I was tempted to go back to London, to disappear into my old life, but something in me believed I could get better. Something was telling me I was better than what I had become. I begged Kieran, my counsellor at the centre, to help me. He looked me in the eyes and asked me, 'Danielle, do you really want this? Really want it?' I swore that I did and he saw the determination in my eyes. I wanted to make something of myself; I felt as if the drugs had robbed me of so many years and I knew I would never grow and change while I was a slave to them.

Just five months ago Kieran brought me to Watford to stay at a home set up by a recovering alcoholic called Lester, who has been sober himself for 14 years. He has two houses – one for guys and one for girls. Both have a live-in recovered addict who knows what we're going through. Right from day one I knew this was a different type of rehabilitation from the one I had just experienced. The treatment meant withdrawing cold turkey – no substitutes or anything, just not touching any type of drug. Lester told us we had to get all of the poison out of our blood in order to be able to deal with the emotions that the drugs were covering up.

The programme is disciplined – we get up at 6.30am and spend time praying and meditating. I had never known God, but have often, even in the hardest places, felt there was someone watching over me. The AA 12-step programme that we follow calls for us to depend on a higher power and to pray to God as we understand him to be. The meditation helps clear our brains of all the clutter of thoughts, then we have a two-hour meeting, learning about the nature of our addictions and the 12-step programme. It has helped me to understand that from a medical point of view, addiction is an illness. It's one that I will always have, but the 12-step principles can help control it. The programme helps you change your patterns of thinking, to move your trust and hope from drugs to a higher power. You have to find something more powerful than your addiction in order to overcome it. I knew by now that I couldn't control it alone and that no partner, family or kids can stop an addict from falling. I started to believe in God and knew that He was the one who would save me from what my life had become.

Darren, who is a recovering alcoholic, lives in the house and he'd become a Christian at the church held in the New Hope day centre. He invited me to his baptism at St Andrew's Church and it all began to make sense to me. When I walked through the door I felt at home. Tears and pain came to the surface, but that felt good and healthy as for so long they'd been repressed. I realised I wanted to say to God that I wanted Him to have all of me, that I wanted to be all that He wanted me to be. I'd been living in darkness, but I wanted to live in the pure light that Jesus was offering me. It felt like making a marriage vow. I was certain about what I wanted; I made a commitment that night to hand my life over to the will and care of God.

It's early days in my faith, but I'm learning loads and it's made my path to recovery much clearer. Since then I've been going to the church at the day centre and I love it. It's so friendly; everyone has made me feel so welcome ever since I arrived. No one criticises you or makes you feel uncomfortable – you just feel accepted and every week you get a chance to say what you think. It has made me realise that it's OK to get down on your hands and knees and pray to God.

I used to want to help people but had nothing to offer them. Now I feel as if I'm becoming less selfish; the hatred, jealousy, resentment and greed are gradually going and I'm becoming more loving. I'm interested in other people again and can actually sit and listen to them – I couldn't even have done that a few months ago.

Drugs have a way of taking over every part of your life. They steal all the good things, all the love, hope, joy and peace. Every dream gets covered in the darkness. Now I'm about to realise a dream from long ago – to go to college and study performing arts. The audition was quite gruelling, but when I got accepted I felt the first rush of confidence that's long been lacking in my life. The college is also going to help me with my maths and English because I missed so much at school. If I can stick at that, I'll have the confidence to go on and do anything.

I work in the gardening project with Elaine twice a week and in the charity shop once a week to keep me busy and to help me give back to the community. I really enjoy it and it's a great chance to spend time with Elaine, who's also one of the leaders at the day centre church.

When I look back at photos taken the day I arrived at Lester's house, it's hard to recognise me as the same person. I was 24, but I look about 16. The thing that strikes me the most is my eyes – they're dark pools, sunk in a pale white face, and they tell the story of what life was like for me then. I was controlled by something that was destroying me; I was lost; I had no hope, no future. Now I know that I'm a child of God and that He loves me. I'll always be an addict, but I believe I can stay off the drugs and make something of my life. It's an amazing feeling to have people who believe in me both here at the house and in the church. I know that they want to be around me, their love for me is real and not based on a drug-induced stupor. Things are getting better with my mum too – we speak regularly and are now friends as well as mother and daughter. We've put each other through a lot, but we love each other too. I'm dealing with the emotional pain that crippled me for so long, and I can honestly say I have hope for my life now. I know now what it's liked to be loved by God and loved by others in His name, and it's given me hope – something that was missing for the first 24 years of my life.

11: Growing pains

You'll use the old rubble of past lives to build anew,
rebuild the foundations from out of your past.
You'll be known as those who can fix anything,
restore old ruins, rebuild and renovate,
make the community livable again.
Isaiah 58:12 *(The Message)*

Of course, over the years in which the events in this book happened, things were growing so rapidly that there were many changes to which Sheila and I as the co-founders had to adjust. I had loved seeing God bring so many amazing people on board to grow New Hope Trust, and yet, where we had been so 'hands on' in the beginning, involved in decisions big and small and able to be with the guys who came most days, suddenly everything was different.

As things changed, my role became more confused, which was difficult both for me and for other members of staff. I still wanted to be involved in so much, but for those whose job it now was to undertake the day-to-day decisions, it was frustrating to have me looking over their shoulder. Everyone does things differently, and seeing other people taking over my roles and not doing them as I would have done them was hard for me. When I had handled the fundraising I always made a point of replying promptly to any gifts that came in to say 'thank you', so I found it hard to sit back when others took much longer to respond than I would have done. It came to the trustees' attention that things were getting difficult, and they suggested I do some personnel development with one of our staff members to try to help things along. Although I tried hard to bring positives to the table as well as constructive criticism, my lack of managerial training and inexperience was evident, and I think the whole thing did more harm than good.

I also got things wrong, and that knocked my confidence. I thought God was saying that the flats at the back of the offices should be turned into a workshop. Others felt it was right that we used them as 'move on' flats and applied for planning permission. I was so sure I knew what God was saying that I did not believe permission would be granted. When it was, I had to eat humble pie. Thankfully, Basil was very gracious to me.

It was a difficult time for me. In some ways it was like having a baby and then being asked to give it away once it was able to walk. I felt out on a limb. In the early days when it was just Sheila, Tim and me, we could pray and make decisions easily. We were all on the same wavelength and so things moved quickly. Now everything (quite rightly) had to go through trustees and committees before decisions were made and action taken. The truth is that the Trust would not be where it is today if we had kept things going like the 'old days'. I started to learn that the greatest success would be if it continued strongly despite the inevitable changes in staff and trustees over the years.

Sheila had felt the time was right for her to move on not long after the new day centre was built. She kindly took on the role of manager there for a while as we recruited someone else, but she knew God was calling her on. With a growing family, it was right that she should be able to spend more time with her grandchildren. When her daughter-in-law died, it was a blessing for her to be free of commitments to be able to give her family the support they needed.

God often asks us to lay one thing down before he gives us another, and this was true in Sheila's case. A few years after she left New Hope Trust, she woke up one morning feeling that God was telling her to go to Peru. She did not even know where Peru was until she got out a map! She spent 14 months working in a prison in Lima where she supported women, some of whom had young babies. She struggled with the language but found that hugs were universally understood, and she soon became a dear friend to all the girls. Sheila was such an important part of the Trust – she had made it happen in so many ways and it was hard to lose her. She has always kept in touch, though, and came to see us and the guys whenever she could as they were like family to her, but I felt a sense of loss at her moving on.

Once Basil had been appointed and we had a good fundraiser in place, I was not sure where I fitted in. Ron was thinking of retiring, all our children had grown up and left home, and so we thought about downsizing our home. After ten years with the Trust I took a six-month sabbatical and we moved to a beautiful village near Beaconsfield. This also meant that I left St Andrew's, where I had been worshipping on and off for 32 years, and started attending our local village church. I tried to throw myself into life there – helping with toddler groups, cream teas for the community, an Alpha course and other local outreach projects, but there was still a gap in my life. I had been working with the homeless for a decade and it was not easy to 'take a break' from it. Being without the guys felt like a bereavement. In fact, I felt God prompt me to grieve the loss of my 'baby' in the sense of giving it to Him to do what He wanted with it. I had to make sure I was not reliant on the Trust and the Trust was not reliant on me.

When the six-month sabbatical was up, the New Hope Trust office was in need of a fundraiser again. So back I went for two years, helping to get new grants and funding for everything from the night shelter through to a summer house for the gardening project to use as an office. I enjoyed being a part of the team again and would also go to New Hope House and to the night shelter to cook meals and to eat with the men staying there. They always appreciated the company and I loved spending time with them.

Once the new fundraiser was happily settled, it was time for me to leave. Once again I was unsettled, unsure of my place in the Trust. On top of this, Ron had started having blackouts and was undergoing vigorous tests to find out what was wrong. He was told it was not cancer, only to find out a few months later that it actually was. The treatment was harsh, as the tumour was near to the facial nerves. He had to have radiotherapy every day for six weeks, plus chemotherapy. This was obviously a very difficult time for us, but thank God the treatment is now finished and Ron has been able to return to work.

At around this time my son Craig was talking to a friend of his, Chris, telling him about the way the Trust had grown and how I was wondering whether God had a role for me there any more. Chris told Craig, 'God's not done with your mum yet,' and when he reported that back to me I felt it was a prophetic word from God. I was really encouraged that God could still use me: even at the age of 62, He was not ready to 'retire' me!

I decided to go back to the day centre and Joy, the new manager there, made me feel really welcome and part of the team. It felt like the right place for me to be – I could be at home to help Ron through his treatment and still have time to spend with the guys at the day centre. There were great opportunities to share my faith, which made me feel so alive again, and I just loved being back in the thick of things, meeting people who needed a friendly ear, and being able to help, even in a small way. As God knew, it was also great preparation for what lay ahead.

The church I was attending was lovely and friendly, but Ron and I were the youngest by a long way and I was starting to feel spiritually dry. With the uncertainty and pain of Ron's illness, I spent a lot of time calling out to God and felt that He said, 'Go to St Andrew's. There's a banquet there; go and have a feast!'

When I went back I found that the church was undergoing extensive refurbishment and so the congregation was dispersing into 'mid-sized community groups' (MSCs). This was an exciting vision, offering church members a chance to explore their own vision for worship, community and outreach. Everyone was invited to join a group local to them which would meet a couple of times a month in places like cafés, school halls and community centres and then return once a month to St Andrew's for a central celebration. Every time the groups were mentioned I sensed the power of God fall on me. Over the years I have noticed that I feel the Holy Spirit in different ways at different times, and yet I always shake when God wants to talk to me about issues that relate to the homeless. I kept thinking, 'Wouldn't it be great if we had an MSC at the New Hope day centre?' It had been my vision for a long time to have a church that was comfortable for the men and women we had met to be in, but we had not found a way to make it work. The staff at the day centre had enough to do without adding to their roles by asking them to lead a church group; we could not do it on a rota basis, as we needed consistency, and we had not found another way. The idea of a smaller group that could be a part of St Andrew's but have its own identity was fantastic, so I started praying for someone else to have the vision as well.

What I did not know was that Elaine, our market garden project manager, had also been thinking and praying about having a church based at the Trust. Her passion to share God's truth and love, as well as her desire to see people healed, had been growing. A number of clients had mentioned to her that they would love the Trust to do some kind of worship service, as they felt that would be a place where they would be comfortable and would not have to worry what others thought of them. One evening Elaine was praying that God would speak to her and show her what He wanted her to do. The next morning I walked into the community home, talking about the idea of an MSC at the day centre! Elaine mentioned it to Viv Maloney, who works at the community home, and she reacted very positively, saying that she and her husband would like to come and chat to us about it. Viv had been working with us for a long time and had prayed for 15 years that we would be able to start a church for the homeless guys, so she was delighted that God was stirring us too.

The four of us met up, sharing our vision and excitement at the idea of starting with an MSC from St Andrew's. We spoke with the leaders of St Andrew's and they came to meet us at the day centre to hear more about it. We said we would love to be a part of the MSC structure, and could they help us with leaders and speakers? They shook their heads. 'That's not how it works. While we will fully support you, God gave you the vision, so you should lead it.'

We were surprised, to say the least! We had never envisaged ourselves as the leaders, and all of us were daunted at the prospect. As we prayed, however, God gave us a picture and the verse from Isaiah 58:12:

> 'You'll use the old rubble of past lives to build anew,
> rebuild the foundations from out of your past.
> You'll be known as those who can fix anything,
> restore old ruins, rebuild and renovate,
> make the community livable again.'

We felt that God had rebuilt our own lives from the rubble and that He was longing to do the same for the people who came to the Trust, so we decided we would go ahead and trust Him for the wisdom and strength to lead. Our hope was, and is, that as people come to know him through the MSC, they will grow in their faith and God will raise them up as leaders and teachers who can go on to form other groups that will reach out into the community.

The easiest part was the location: we already had the day centre, and the trustees of New Hope were happy for us to use it on a Sunday, so we started to meet to pray in February 2005. We were so nervous, we actually had a week's trial run before we went ahead and opened it up to everyone else!

We kept things quite informal to make everyone feel at home, and the emphasis is on loving one another and making everyone feel welcome. The guys love the fact that they are coming to the day centre, a place where they feel at home, and so they do not come in worrying that they will do the wrong thing at the wrong time. We start with coffee, cake and chat, so there is a real family feel, and we keep the services interactive so that everyone gets involved. We have worship and one of us, usually Elaine or Paul (Viv's husband), will give a short message from the Bible, then we go on to discuss it. There is a chance for everyone to air their views, to voice their thoughts, concerns and questions, and we also spend time in prayer together when everyone can be honest about their needs.

Once a month we go back to St Andrew's Church and, because everyone feels a part of the MSC, they feel more comfortable at St Andrew's. Every three months our MSC is on duty to serve, so we welcome people as they arrive at St Andrew's, serve tea and coffee and take up the collection. The members of our MSC love being involved and feel a real sense of privilege in being asked to undertake these tasks. The congregation at St Andrew's also enjoys the chance to meet some of the people from our MSC; it often blows away the stereotypes when they chat to those who have been homeless or hear their testimonies from the front. Since the MSC has started we have had the privilege of seeing four of our members baptised at St Andrew's, all giving powerful testimonies of how Jesus has changed their lives.

Tim is one of those who has been baptised, and it has been such a privilege for us to see him on his journey to faith. He became homeless at the age of 59 and the New Hope Trust outreach team took him to the night shelter. Having been anti-religion for many years, he was pleased to find that no one forced their faith on him and he gradually became more interested in Jesus, and even asked for a Bible to read. When we started the MSC he came to our first official meeting and has been a committed member ever since. He describes his journey as 'being led from a world of self-created darkness towards meaning and light for the first time', and is now passionately evangelical about his faith, encouraging others not to leave it as late as he did to give their lives to God. We have loved seeing the change in him and he delights in encouraging other members of the MSC in their own journeys of faith.

After a year we started a home group every Tuesday at Paul and Viv's house, which is another chance to get together, pray for one another, read the Bible, learn and grow in a comfortable environment.

The vision that the St Andrew's leadership team had for the MSCs has given us all a wonderful opportunity. There are now 26 different MSCs with more than 1,400 people involved, meeting anywhere from coffee shops to Scout huts, and more are planned to come on board. I love the opportunity we have been given to take Jesus into the world and then come back to the church centre for teaching, refreshment and encouragement. It has stretched us all beyond our wildest dreams, and we are so grateful that God equips when He calls! The promise of God was that His presence would go with us (Exodus 33:14), and He certainly has kept His promise.

The desire for our MSC is to do more to reach out to those who are not even ready to come to the day centre as a form of church yet. We have linked up with a local church, Soul Survivor Watford, to get a team together who may go into the night shelter once a week and offer to listen to anyone who wants to chat and to pray with them if they would like. We know that we cannot do it all on our own and, as with the work of New Hope Trust, we hope that our outreach work to church and disciple people from the streets will cover many denominations and get lots of local worshippers on board.

As an MSC leadership we have also been really inspired by Lester and his houses for recovering addicts, which have helped people like Danielle. We would love to follow Lester's example and have a home where recovering drug addicts and alcoholics could be supported with a discipleship course. We have seen many times over the years that it is very hard for people to change their way of life when they are surrounded by people who have the same bad habits as they do. They need a safe place where everyone is supporting them in their desire to be clean and sober.

We know, too, that the real hope for people's lives is to know Jesus. As the one who made us, God is the best person to put us back together again when we are broken. We would like to get others from different churches involved as mentors to provide one-on-one ongoing support and spiritual input. A house where we could combine the stability and facilities which homeless people so desperately need with the support of a good rehabilitation programme and the love of Jesus is the best that we can offer, and we hope to make it a reality in the coming years.

The years 2005 and 2006 have been the most exciting and yet the most challenging since the early days of the coaches. The joy and excitement of being involved with the MSC has been fantastic. As I write, it was just last night that we had some 20 men and women at the MSC and a real sense of God's presence with us. A new visitor gave his life to Jesus, while his friend recommitted herself to God. One guy came in full of rage and was so angry with God. By the end of the evening his heart had been warmed, all the anger had disappeared from his face and he looked positively serene.

While all these wonderful things have happened through the MSC and I have been greatly encouraged, there have also been some very difficult things running alongside in my personal life. The reality is that suffering touches all of us, regardless of any plans we have, and my real 'thorn in the flesh' throughout my adult life has been my health. As I mentioned earlier, I had breast cancer and since then have suffered on and off with colitis (a painful inflammation of the bowel).

While things have been taking off with the MSC, my health has been deteriorating. I started getting pains in my chest and thought perhaps it was bad indigestion. Because of my colitis, I have a routine check-up every two years. The consultant advised me to get my doctor to check my gastric tract. While doing this he also, unusually, did an ultrasound scan which picked up a swelling. I had been feeling unwell for a number of months, as though I was constantly fighting a cold, and after many tests, scans and a biopsy I have been diagnosed with liver cancer. Unless chemotherapy can shrink the tumour, it is inoperable, but – thank God – the cancer has spread no further. Although it was a shock to receive the diagnosis, I was also relieved, because not knowing was harder for me. It has been a very strange time, as Ron has just finished his treatment for cancer of the nasal pharynx and now I am starting my own treatment.

A few months ago one of the new Christians at our MSC, Darren, felt God had said to him that there were steep hills for me to climb and when I got weary, God would pick me up and carry me. How right that picture has been. During my darkest times I have felt God carry me, comfort me and encourage me, and give me strength for today and hope for tomorrow with a real sense of purpose for the future. Our God is amazing!

I firmly believe that no matter what life throws at us, both good and bad, the most important thing is that we focus on God. He is our strength; He is our hope. If we trust in ourselves we will not get very far, but in the brightest day and even in the darkest night, His love and strength can guide us. I continue to worship God in my current circumstances, I trust that He will heal me and I look forward to whatever plans God has for me in the future. So often we see what the enemy means for evil being turned round by God and used for good.

I am very glad that both New Hope Trust and the MSC are in such safe hands while I am having my treatment, and so thankful that God helped me to lay it all down before Him. We have found it very helpful to remember throughout our work with the homeless that this has most definitely been God's work and not our own. I was never reminded of this more clearly than when, one day at the coaches, one of the guys, John, who had become a Christian, said to Sheila and me, 'Aren't you good that you started this up?'

Barry, who had only been a Christian for a few months himself, quite rightly said, 'If Janet and Sheila hadn't done it, God would have found another way.'

We know this is true. God did not use Sheila and me because we were holier than others, more gifted, more anointed or more capable than anyone else. He used us because we were willing. We made ourselves available to Him, took Him at His word and wanted to follow wherever He led, inspired by all that Jesus had done in our lives to give us a 'hope and a future'. We give all the glory to God.

Practical advice

We have always felt that the work of New Hope Trust is easily replicable. If you have a group of praying Christians, a building and a vision, then what has been done for the homeless in Watford could be done for the homeless in any town, or in fact for any other group in our needy society. This section provides some practical advice and sets out some of the things we have learned along the way which may help you as you follow God's call.

Prayer

We cannot overemphasise that prayer is and always has been the lifeblood of what we do. Every step we took was covered in prayer, which became so easy as we saw God opening doors and answering prayers beyond our wildest dreams. As we had a hunger to read the Bible, God would give us verses to encourage, chastise and prepare us for the things to come. Every time God gave us a verse I dated it in my Bible. It was great to be able to hold on to a verse when all was looking so bleak at the time.

We have a monthly early morning prayer session attended by just a few, and also monthly prayer and praise meetings alternating around the projects. Each individual project prays daily for the work of the Trust.

Vision

Keep to your original God-given vision. Over the years you may add to it by all means after prayer, but do not be tempted to water it down. If God has called the work into being, then He has to be central to all you do. Prayerful staff, volunteers and trustees are essential. Be humble – remember this is about God, not about you, and without the presence of the Holy Spirit it will just be a good work and will not necessarily extend the kingdom of God.

Many people with whom you come into contact will be open to spiritual matters and would like to be prayed with or for. Listen to the Holy Spirit and be bold and open to these God-given opportunities. Others will have no interest, so respect their views too. Just love them and be Jesus to them.

We have always believed that Jesus would give the homeless the best, and we have always worked on this principle. All our projects are well furnished and inviting. This also means that the guys in general respect the project and have a sense of ownership and therefore take care of what they have.

Love

All who are called to such a ministry need a genuine love for all the men and women with whom they come into contact. People are quick to spot a 'do-gooder' and, unsurprisingly, do not respond well to being patronised.

Tough love can be very important, and I have to confess that I have not always been very good at it, which is why I needed the balance of Sheila, who is fantastic in this respect! Loving someone is not always about saying 'yes' and giving them the easy option: sometimes you have to think of yourself as a parent disciplining a child for their own good. Again, this has to be done out of a genuine love and not a need to gain power on your part.

It is wise to watch boundaries between staff and the people they are helping. It is very easy for someone who is in a vulnerable situation to confuse the love they are shown through such a project with a romantic love or a love they come to depend on too much. Make sure everyone involved in the project is aware of this issue and keeps the highest standards of personal integrity.

Do not get disillusioned if, after weeks of devoted support to a person, he or she relapses and lets you down. It will happen time and time again, so you need to work hard at not becoming cynical. God is merciful and so should we be. Sometimes we have to let people go and pray that either they will return or God will provide someone else to support and encourage them. Often we are called simply to sow the seeds, and we do not always have the joy of reaping; at other times we are reaping what others have sown.

Unity

Getting the local churches on board has been key for us. We went along to Churches Together meetings, which encourage Christians to work together, and would share the vision with all the members of the Watford group to get them and their churches on board. We made ourselves known within the local community by taking any opportunity to speak at a church or local group, whether it was Christian or secular. Getting stories into the local paper also helped raise our profile, so we used opportunities like a sleepout on the streets to highlight the problem of homelessness, and took annual opportunities like Harvest festivals, Christmas and when particularly bad weather was forecast to get information out and encourage people to get involved with our work.

It is also important that you do not work in isolation. If there is another group doing something similar in your area, then go and visit their project. This will help you to ascertain whether your project can meet needs that are not already being met and to make sure you do not replicate work being done by others. It will also help you to work out ways in which you can support and encourage one another. Small gestures such as attending other groups' AGMs are usually much appreciated and show you are supportive of their work.

There are also usually statutory bodies working on similar projects with which you can get involved and from which you can learn. They sometimes provide free training for small groups and can help strengthen you in areas of weakness.

Accountability

Be accountable. One of the best ways to do this is to apply for charitable status very quickly. This reassures people that you are working to strict guidelines and rules for the running of your activities. Becoming an official charity places obligations on your trustees and means that you will have to prepare accounts annually and make them available to anyone who wants to see them, as well as complying with many legal requirements. Appoint trustees who have the same vision and values for the project and can bring varied experience and expertise to your work.

Working with your local council/politicians

Local councillors often run Saturday morning surgeries, and we found that when we were applying for project planning permission it really helped to go to these surgeries to back up the written applications and put a face to our letters.

Working with all the local political parties was also essential, so we invited each of them to come and visit our projects and attend events, and we also attended the community functions they were putting on.

Get to know your local mayor and MP and invite them to join you in a personal tour of your work, ending with lunch at one of the projects with the residents. You will be amazed at what a positive impact this can have on both the visitor and the residents. We have had many requests from residents to have a photograph taken with the mayor wearing his or her chain of office so that they can send it to their family! The acceptance and interest shown by local dignitaries can be a real boost.

You may be able to get an inroad into central government through your local MP, which will help you to speak up for the homeless and the problems you have seen first hand in your community.

Planning permission

Most building projects will need planning permission, but do not be daunted by this process. Meet with the planning officers as soon as you have identified the building you want. This will give you an opportunity to tell them about your plans, get them excited about your project and hear what they have to say. The planning officers put the recommendations to the council members, so they are very important, as, of course, are the people who live near the building or the local shops and businesses. It is a good idea to go and visit every neighbour before they receive the planning notice (which will happen shortly after you submit your request). Again, this gives you an opportunity to share your plans, alleviate any fears they may have and reassure them that you are always at the end of the telephone in the unlikely event that there is any trouble.

When the project is up and running, invite them round to meet your clients. This has worked well for us, and one neighbour even regularly baked cakes for the guys and girls after her visit!

Volunteers

Without volunteers, most charities cannot exist, so make sure they feel valued. It is a good idea to have regular get-togethers and prayer times so they know about everything that is going on and you can share the ups and downs in confidence. We currently have more than 100 volunteers who are managed by a part-time volunteer coordinator. If possible you can use the clients as volunteers, as this does a huge amount for their self-esteem. Trust them and, in general, they will not let you down.

As you grow, do not expect everyone to be prepared to work 12 hours a day just because you do. Most folk will work eight hours; if they do more, make sure they know how much you appreciate it and do not get critical or resentful. We know it happens, because we have been there!

Some of your volunteers may be a bit nervous at first, so allay their anxieties by making things easy for them. Encourage them to come and serve a cup of tea – something that will ease them into the project gently and make them feel as if they have made a difference when they realise that a smile and a warm welcome go a long way.

As the work grows, the founders can no longer oversee everything and need to be able to delegate and trust their staff and volunteers. This can be hard at first, but try to be involved without interfering, and encourage a healthy, united, empowered team to grow.

Fundraising

I love it! Prayer was again the foundation to our fundraising as God inspired me to write an appropriate letter, approach the right person at the right time and build up a database of supporters. Always say 'thank you' immediately – and not just with a standard letter, but with a personal one. Give the donors feedback on the project and mention anything that you know personally about them if it is relevant. Tell them about success stories and give information about how their money will be spent. Send regular information letters just to keep in touch, not only to ask for money, and send a Christmas card.

Record donations and expenditure meticulously so that your accounts are in good working order for the Charity Commission, your trustees and your supporters.

Get streetwise

One of the ways to do this is to learn from the guys and girls with whom you are working. One of the best training sessions I have ever been to – about anger management and conflict resolution – was presented by a resident from his own life experience.

As you grow, there are also charities that are happy to give funds for training purposes. The Directory of Social Change have an excellent training and fundraising section and most local CVSs will let you use their Funder Finder software and provide some good training courses.

Publicity

Get to know the reporter on your local paper who deals with your area. Invite them to visit the project and phone them when you have an interesting story to tell or at key times of year, such as winter for homeless projects. Our community fundraiser has got to know the reporter from our local paper (the *Watford Observer*), so much so that at this year's fundraising sleepout, the reporter joined the 250 supporters sleeping on the streets of Watford to find out first hand what it would be like to be homeless. This, of course, added a new touch of reality to his article and gained more local interest in both the charity and the problem of homelessness in the area.

Charity shop

A charity shop is a good way of raising funds, and ours has proven to be so much more too. We have designated a chapel area and many folk have been prayed for, Christians and non-Christians. Our shop is a service to the community as well as to the homeless. The Christian music played generates a very peaceful atmosphere. Most volunteers are trained on site, and you must comply with all trading standards (find the Trading

Standards number in your local telephone directory), including health and safety issues. Some training is free from your local CVS, so speak to them as they are very keen to support volunteer groups.

Final word

Again we come back to prayer and listening to the still, small voice. If you believe that God has spoken to you, check it out, take a risk and be bold; you never know where God might take you. Today New Hope Trust is the main provider of services to the homeless in south-west Hertfordshire, and it all started with reading the words of Isaiah 58. May God bless you as you step out in faith. We know you will have the privilege of meeting many angels on the way who will surely enrich your life.

Contact us

If you would like to find out more or visit our services, please visit our website at www.newhope.org.uk for contact details and information.

Acknowledgements

It has been a real privilege to recount this amazing work of God, and we hope so much that you will be encouraged and inspired by what the Lord has done – not only in the work of New Hope Trust, but in our own lives as well.

It has been impossible to cover all that the Lord has done over these past 18 years. Many of our staff and volunteers have their own amazing stories to tell and we hope they will forgive us for not being able to share them all. However, our thanks go to all the staff and volunteers who have contributed to the story and to all our supporters past and present; without you all there would be no New Hope Trust. Our thanks also to Colin Bullimore and all at St Mary's for the inspiration of the Tower Club, where everything began.

We are grateful to all those who have shared their experiences and testimonies, and we have changed some names to protect family and friends.

Our grateful thanks to Tim Robson, who has supported us from the beginning and has worked tirelessly for the Trust and the homeless over the years. Our thanks also to our families, who have allowed us to share their stories.

Our thanks to Valerie Perkes, who urged us to write the story down, to Richard Herkes at Kingsway for guiding us on the way, and to Liza Hoeksma for her sensitivity as she collated the stories and met with many angels past and present. Thanks also to Emma and Craig Borlase, Emily Layzell, Karen Layzell, Simon Nicholls, David and Jenny Rosser, Becca Sampson and Emily Vesey for reading the script and making helpful contributions.

And, of course, our overwhelming thanks to the Lord, without Whom none of this story would be possible. We thank him for His faithfulness in the past and trust Him for the future.

To God be the glory; great things he has done.
Janet Hosier and Sheila Meaning